I0491473

Accounting for Small Business Owners

*Learn the Basics and Principles of Accounting
(Even for Complete Beginners)*

Chris Walton

implied. Readers acknowledge that the author is not engaging in the rendering of legal, financial, medical or professional advice. The content within this book has been derived from various sources. Please consult a licensed professional before attempting any techniques outlined in this book.

By reading this document, the reader agrees that under no circumstances is the author responsible for any losses, direct or indirect, which are incurred as a result of the use of the information contained within this document, including, but not limited to, — errors, omissions, or inaccuracies.

Table of Contents

Your Free Gift

GET YOUR FREE PRINTABLE CHECKLIST EXCLUSIVE FOR YOU

As a way of saying thanks for your purchase, I'm offering you a Free Checklist that's exclusive to readers of Accounting for Small Business Owners. This is a printable checklist that serves as a guide of all the exercises and the action items you can use and implement. Use this checklist as a reminder and a guide for what you learned in the book

CLICK HERE TO DOWNLOAD YOUR FREE GIFT

Introduction

I feel you. Running a business can be overwhelming and stressful. I get it. Accounting can be complicated, but in this book, I will simplify it for you so you can start getting results immediately. If you are planning on starting a business, or you are interested in the subject this book is for you.

Ever heard the saying "it's never too late"? Well... it's not true, especially when it comes to accounting. Your business could suffer huge losses if you don't have the accounting skills necessary to detect malpractice, such as fraud and pilferage. Over time it gets confusing and frustrating to you and everyone involved. So it's very important to learn the skills of accounting that you need to develop as a business owner as early as possible, or you will miss out on one of the most valuable skills for running a business. It is crucial that you don't delay learning accounting. Your business will thank you.

For example, do you have an idea that many businesses like yours are always under the constant threat of collapse? In case you are wondering, it's very true that imminent threats of failure are always lurking. In fact, many small businesses don't make it past the startup stage. Not only that, but are you confident that you are sufficiently equipped with the business skills required to overcome operational challenges and achieve growth? I know you have the answer to this question, but the key issues I have highlighted in this introduction will help you tell if you are right or wrong.

To begin with, the high rate of failures among small businesses has become a big problem. Startups are failing at alarming rates and more established businesses are not spared either. According to McIntyre (2018), first-year and second-year failure rates of small business startups average 20 percent and 30 percent, respectively. The situation is even worse with businesses that have been around for 5 and 10 years, because they suffer failure rates of 50 percent and 70 percent, respectively (McIntyre, 2018).

That brings us to the big question: what could be the root causes of the high rate of small business failures? Although there have been varied opinions about this, it can't be denied that lack of accounting knowledge among small business owners ranks high among the leading causes of these failures. There is no doubt that lack of accounting skills makes it difficult for small business owners to manage debt levels, track inventories, monitor profit trends, detect fraud, and weed out operational inefficiencies, among other crucial functions. This leaves businesses exposed to overwhelming challenges that eventually lead to failure.

To put this into perspective, let me share with you Paul Pruitt's September 9, 2016, motivational story in the *Entrepreneur* website about his fall from grace. After launching his real estate agency startup in the mid-1990s, Pruitt quickly scaled the heights of success and transformed his business into a profitable, multimillion entity within less than 10 years. But the good tidings didn't last long. According to Pruitt (2016) his success came to an abrupt end in 2008 after the business went under with $3 million in debt. In his own admission, Pruitt (2016) regretted the decision to delegate the management of the business to his family members. It was one of the family members that siphoned all funds from the company's bank account (Pruitt, 2016). As such, Pruitt was left with no option but to close down the business.

So, what lessons can we learn from Pruitt's unfortunate experience? I would say without hesitation that this was clearly a case fraud that Pruitt failed to detect. In fact, the other important bit that I picked from Pruitt's story was his admission that he was obsessed with the sales and marketing function in his business above everything else (2016). Now, you make the connection there; no mention of accounting. And it's no wonder fraud happened right under his nose. Accounting knowledge would have helped Pruitt to promptly detect the fraudulent withdrawal of funds from his business' bank account. The statement of cash flows would have provided him the details of inward and outward movement of money in the bank account.

You cannot run short of evidence from past experiences that underscore the need for sound accounting practices in your small business. An infographic prepared by Wallace (2013) shed light on some of the businesses that were considered to face high risks of failure. This included independent restaurants, retail stores, and direct sales. In his verdict, Wallace (2013) observed that independent restaurants faced risks of failure because the owners lacked business skills despite having abundant skills of their craft. He also mentioned the need for the owners of independent restaurants to have the knowhow to raise capital for their businesses in order to have realistic chances of survival.

In an article he authored in *Forbes*, Andriole (2018) similarly apportioned the blame of high rates of business failures to lack of knowhow of funding dynamics among entrepreneurs. According to him, there are cases where entrepreneurs do not look beyond their circles of families and friends when seeking funding. Some of those who do seek funding from outside sources, they hardly understand the techniques for committing the funds to viable investments. There are entrepreneurs that cannot even attach proper valuations of their investments (Andriole, 2008). If you look keenly at the issues raised by both Wallace (2013) and Andriole (2018), they have everything to do with accounting. These issues actually touch on the financing and budgeting aspects of accounting.

Taking into consideration all the facts that I have highlighted so far, do you still feel confident about your readiness to manage the financial aspects of your business effectively? If you are not confident about it, then here is a chance. You are not alone in this situation. There are many entrepreneurs like you that are doing so well in many aspects of their businesses, but still face the challenges of accounting for their business activities. I urge you to not find consolation in this unwelcome reality; it's actually a wakeup call. Do not let your lack of accounting knowledge prevail any longer because there is so much at stake about securing the future of your business.

That is the reason I have written this book to help you acquire accounting skills and apply them right away to your business. This is a step by step actionable book. I won't promise to make you an expert on the topic but I promise to simplify accounting for you so you can apply it. This book will help you run your business better no matter what your background is or what industry you're in.

The step by step accounting principles basics and tools that you're about to read are proven to yield incredible results for small business owners of all backgrounds and industries, Every chapter in this book will help you overcome your misunderstanding and confusion about accounting. If you follow the training in this book, it is very likely that you will never have to worry about accounting skills ever again.

Commit yourself to this learning process with the ultimate goal of assuming total control over your financial reporting activities. The ability to prepare, interpret, or query financial data will give you the leverage you need to detect errors in your financial reports or to provide guidance to your accounting staff. You will also be in a more knowledgeable position to engage your suppliers, customers, lenders, government agencies, and investors on all matters concerning your financial reporting and the overall health of your business.

With my help and expertise, you will be fully equipped with the skills and knowledge you need to be able to take your small business from confusion and stress to easy flow, growth, and profit. People thank me for how my consulting services have changed their life, and continuously help them understand and leverage accounting for their lives and businesses. This is the exact same knowledge that I will be unveiling in this book. It's easy for anyone to get results with. It doesn't have to be hard, complicated and confusing.

Chapter One:
Accounting for Small Business

Now that you are here, it's my belief that you are taking that important step to learn accounting. But like any other learner attempting a new thing, I know you might be experiencing a bit of anxiety. There's that big question lingering over your mind: where do you start? I remember having the same feeling when I stepped into a car for my first driving lesson. But luckily, my instructor was at hand to guide me through the initial steps. You are not alone either. I'll be guiding you through the initial steps and all the way until the end of this book.

To begin with, what is your attitude towards accounting? Well, I guess you have a favorable perception of it, now that you are interested in acquiring the skill. But if you still have some doubt lingering in your head about how simple or difficult accounting is, I would say that it is absolutely understandable.

Back in the days when I was studying business in college, the majority of my classmates flocked to the marketing and human resource management majors because they felt accounting was a bit tough. For those of us who majored in accounting, not only did we enjoy the privilege of being smaller classes, we also found the subject extremely simple and exciting! So, sweep all those doubts away and let's get down to business!

In this chapter, we will be focusing on the basic accounting terms and how they relate to business operations. We will be looking at those initial stages of accounting so that you can understand what accounting generally entails. Let me tease your mind a bit with this question: how would you define accounting? Sounds a tough question for now... doesn't it? But I know you have an idea because you are in business already.

Accounting is more or less a routine activity that helps you keep track of the overall progress of your business. Therefore, when accounting for your small business, you will be using the recommended procedures to record, measure, classify, and interpret financial data. Your primary aim here will be to generate financial reports.

Although it is common for people to use the terms accounting and bookkeeping interchangeably, don't make that mistake. Don't assume the two mean the same thing. Bookkeeping simply involves recording and storing the data for your business transactions. Accounting has more to do with summarizing, presenting, analyzing, and interpreting the recorded data. Therefore, bookkeeping is more or less a discipline of accounting and not its equivalent.

In bookkeeping, you will find the cash ledger useful in recording any cash transactions, be it receipts or payments. You'll list all the items you have sold either on cash or credit in the sales summary. The purchases summary contains all the items you bought either on cash or credit. Accounts receivable tracks debtors to whom you sold products on credit. Accounts payable are the amounts you owe others for credit purchases. The inventory summarizes the inward and outward movement of products in your business. Payroll costs, owner's drawings, and loans outstanding are the other entries that you are likely to encounter in a bookkeeper's general ledger.

Understanding Bookkeeping Methods

The single entry method and the double entry method are both acceptable in bookkeeping. However, you should find more comfort in the latter because it highlights the consequences of any given transaction to all the respective accounts. The idea behind the double entry bookkeeping is that for any entry that you post to a given account, there has to be an opposite impact to a different account. For example, you need to record a credit purchase as a debit entry in the Creditors' A/C. But you still need to record the amount as a credit entry in the Accounts Payable A/C. This way, you will have acknowledged an increase in your creditors' liabilities, and an increase in your outstanding payables liabilities as well.

How to Post a Double Entry

A double entry affects your assets, liability, income, expenses, and equity (capital) accounts. You will debit a spike in assets and credit a dip in assets. For changes in liability, debit is a fall and credit a rise. You will account for your growth of income with a credit entry and recognize a dip in income with debit entry. As for your expense account, you will debit an increase and credit a decline. Change in equity or capital requires that you debit a decline and credit an increase.

For example, the entries for the purchase of a vehicle by check and cash sale of 10 bales of baking flour will be as follows.

Vehicle purchase by check:

Debit	Vehicle	Asset increase
Credit	Bank	Asset decline

Cash sale of 10 bales of baking flour:

Debit	Cash	Asset increase
Credit	Inventory	Asset decrease

Insights Into Accounting Methods

You will be using either the cash-based or the accrual-based method in your small business accounting. The cash-basis accounting method involves recognizing your revenue at the time of receipt. Similarly, you recognize a payment the moment you release the money. This is a simple and straight-to-the-point method of accounting because it only recognizes the actual inflow or outflow of cash transactions.

Application of the cash-basis accounting is best suited for your business if you do not keep an inventory. You will also find this method useful when in need of changing the timing of the actual inflow or outflow of cash. This helps reduce your tax liability for that accounting period. You will basically be deferring your income tax liability if you change the receipt of cash to a later date.

Accrual-basis accounting, on the other hand, involves recognizing revenue immediately after earning it and recognizing an expense soon after incurring it. This means recording your credit sales and purchases as receipts and payments, alongside cash sales and purchases. This would be the recommended method for you to use if you keep an inventory because it captures the impact of a transaction on its destination account (either asset or liability account) and on the opposite account as well.

If you plan to subject your financial reports to auditing, the Generally Accepted Accounting Principles (GAAP) recommend the use of the accrual basis accounting method. That's because it uses the matching principle to weigh revenue against expenses in the same accounting period.

How to Record an Accrual Basis Accounting Entry
Record a credit sale soon after you dispatch an invoice to your customer. Post a journal entry debiting your debtor's account and crediting your sales account. This entry captures an increase in the accounts receivable asset and decrease in the inventory asset. Similarly, record a purchase soon after you receive an invoice from your supplier. Post a journal entry debiting your purchases account and crediting your creditor's account. This entry captures an increase in inventory asset and an increase in the accounts payable liability.

Quiz: Which of the following statements is false?

a) Bookkeeping is part of accounting.
b) Accounting is part of bookkeeping.
c) Both.

Closing the Accounting Period

During closing you will ideally be removing any amounts from temporary accounts—that is, the income and expense accounts—of the income statement so as to begin the next accounting period with zero balances. The process involves making closing entries that move the end of period balances from the income statement to the balance sheet. Closing of accounts also sets the stage for preparation of financial statements. It ensures that you will have only new entries in your income statement for the succeeding period.

Inventory Management Tips

You have been in business for a while now, haven't you? I guess you have been depleting your inventory and replenishing it regularly. That means you are familiar with issues that concern tracking your inventory. The only difference could be that you haven't been giving any particular attention to the way your inventory affects the financial reporting and other operational parameters of your business. It is important to account for every aspect of your inventory, as we are going to see in the discussion below.

Inventory is the physical count of production materials and the finished or the unfinished items for sale. It is a current asset that counts toward your sales and helps you determine gross profit and working capital trends. The key factors you should consider when evaluating your inventory are: evidence of economic value, designation as materials for direct consumption in production operations, and availability for sale as finished products in the immediate or near future. That means your inventory doesn't include inconsumable assets—such as tools and equipment—that are meant to facilitate your production processes.

Classify Your Inventory
Classify your inventory using categories such as raw materials, work in process, and finished merchandise. All the inputs consumed during production to create end products count toward raw materials. Such raw materials may also include ingredients that either transform or aid transformation of your inputs into finished products. For example, milk would be obviously the main raw material for your dairy processing business. However, other items like stationary, additives, preservatives, and packaging will form part of your raw materials as well. The nature

and scope of raw materials will always vary with the type of your small business.

Work in process (WIP) consists of inventory items you have not certified as complete and ready for sale. All the products that are at different levels of processing or approval should fall under this category. WIP also includes goods with manufacturing defects and waste from your production processes. Large quantities of WIP goods in your stores generally indicate a flourishing business with a high number of customer orders or production targets. However, they could also signal production inefficiencies occasioned by delays in your production lines.

Finished goods are the desired outputs generated by your production system. Such goods are ready for sale or dispatch to target market destinations. Finished goods will always remain in your inventory until you complete the sale and/or delivery transactions with your customers. Sample products and inward returns from customers also count toward your inventory of finished goods.

Select the Appropriate Inventory System

When accounting for your inventory, you will basically be apportioning the different costs associated with the inventory. Such costs include sales tax, returns inward, returns outward, storage fees, and packaging costs among others. Returns inward and returns outward are costs incurred when goods (damaged or rejected) are returned to you or when you return goods to your supplier. These costs will similarly feature in your computations for the cost of goods sold (COGS).

You have to prepare appropriate general ledger entries to account for the inventory costs. Ensure that you debit the relevant accounts that are affected by a cost entry. For example, a sales tax will affect the sales and accounts payable. The costing process is much easier if you have an automated inventory management system in place because the costs will automatically be allocated to the respective ledger accounts.

The type of your inventory accounting system is determined by the frequency of your stock counts and the complexity of the tools you use. You may choose the periodic inventory system which simply involves using a spreadsheet to track inward and outward movement of items from your store or shelves. This particular type of inventory accounting system is performed weekly, monthly, quarterly, and annually. Many small businesses find this system convenient because it is not financially burdening.

Alternatively, you may install a perpetual inventory accounting system that provides built-in capabilities for monitoring sales and purchase deliveries in real time. That means the inventory count will be a continuous rather than a periodically scheduled process. The perpetual system is more sophisticated and accurate because it involves the deployment of bar code scanning and an automated accounting platform. The conveniences and strategic benefits of this type of inventory accounting system compensate the costs associated with its acquisition, installation, and maintenance.

Keep Monitoring Your Inventory

Although it may sound routine, inventory management plays a crucial role in the achievement of your small business operations goals and overall growth strategy. The dynamics associated with inventory management requires your business to have continuous evaluation capabilities and robust monitoring structures. You need the ability to identify fast moving and stagnant inventory items to be in a better position to determine your production priorities. It is about being able to decide the inventory items that must be increased and the ones that must be scaled down to enhance both operational and strategic efficiency.

The process of managing the inventory primarily seeks to minimize the levels of idle inventory, while simultaneously preventing its depletion. The idea is to maintain your inventory at levels that are sufficient to efficiently support your scheduled production operations. For example, a bloated inventory level can potentially lead to the misrepresentation of financial information related to your sales. This shows the way inventory management helps you achieve efficiency in your entire supply chain. It also allows you to maintain accuracy in the presentation of your financial reports.

Trends of your turnover ratio are useful in monitoring efficiency. You will probably find the ratio of your profit turnover margins—that is, the amount of net income relative to net sales—helpful in determining the profitability associated with particular inventory items. In fact, this is one of the key metrics that an investor or a lender will scrutinize when evaluating the operations and growth potential of your small business.

Embrace Relevant Techniques and Approaches

There are various techniques that you can deploy in your inventory management. You may consider using the economic order quantity (EOQ), which by the way stands out as one the widely used inventory management techniques. When using EOQ, you will be able to tell in advance the material components or unit items that you should order in large quantities to minimize your frequency of replenishing the inventory of those particular items. This way, you would be restricting bulk purchases to items that are required in large quantities to sustain your production or operations.

The just-in-time approach to inventory management is similarly common, especially in production operations. This technique allows you to schedule your orders of raw materials to match specific quantities required for particular production operations. This eliminates the need of keeping large quantities of inventory in your stores. The approach is useful for freeing up your cash rather than tying it down to the acquisition and storage of unnecessary inventory items.

Demand forecasting involves using past trends of sales to estimate the quantities of goods that you need to keep in your inventory. You must have sufficient understanding of the seasonal fluctuations in the trends of demand for your goods to be able to deploy this technique effectively.

The safety stock inventory is the other technique that is at your disposal. It is a cautious approach that involves keeping stock that exceeds the projected demand to provide backup against sudden spike in demand. You will find this technique helpful if you want to avoid depleting your stocks prematurely, especially in a business environment where demand fluctuations are rife.

Widespread use of ecommerce has brought the dropshipping inventory technique to prominence. This technique eliminates the need for the physical storage because you get to fulfill customer orders without coming in contact with the goods. It is a situation where you ship goods directly from the supplier to the customer. These are the kinds of arrangements that are witnessed in ecommerce sites when customers make purchases online.

Common Inventory Valuation Methods

The inventory is one of the accounts you must close at the end of each reporting period. You need valuation to establish the COGS and the subsequent profits or losses related to inventory. As such, you will be looking at the amount of money you spent to acquire and transform your inventory in addition to calculating the value of the remaining inventory. You will be able to estimate your profitability when you weigh this amount against the total sales for the period. There are different types of inventory valuation methods, and your choice of any particular method will have an impact on your overall profit margins.

The first in, first out (FIFO) valuation method involves prioritizing the oldest items in your inventory when releasing raw materials for production or goods for sale. For example, if you received $100 worth of stationery supplies today, you will have to clear the previous stationery items in your inventory prior to touching any item in the newly delivered batch. You will base your inventory valuation on the quantity and purchase pricing of the remaining inventory.

The FIFO method will present you numerous advantages, especially when there is inflation. The fact that you are releasing older items that had lower prices prior to inflation means that inventory is generating more value for your business during your COGS calculation. It results in lower costs of goods sold which, in turn, generates higher gross profits when subtracted from sales. FIFO is widely recommended for use because it is flexible in terms of ensuring that old inventory is cleared from your store. You do not have to worry about expiry dates and loss of value of your inventory due to weather elements and passage of time.

Last in, first out (LIFO) is the opposite of FIFO. In it, the recently delivered items are issued ahead of the items that were previously in your store or shelves. Using the stationery example above, you will have to clear items in the newly delivered inventory before touching the items that were there before. Just as is the case with the FIFO method, you will base your valuation on the quantity and purchase pricing of the remaining items.

The LIFO method is similarly designed for deployment during periods of inflation. Generally, inflation triggers an increase in the prices of items over time. This means that the inventory you purchased recently will be costlier than the previous ones. As such, you will be seeking to offset the impact of inflation by issuing the higher-priced inventories first so that they can be part of your calculation for your COGS. This way, you will be able to reduce your profits for the period and thereby attract a lower tax liability. But be cautious before choosing this method. There are inventory items that could remain in your business for a very long time and end up expiring or losing value.

There is also the weighted average cost (WAC) valuation method that helps you distinguish between the amount of money you allocate toward inventory and the amount that you allocate toward COGS. You will find this method useful when compounded with the challenge of separating and tracking the unit costs of different items in your inventory. You have to calculate WAC for each item by dividing the total value of your inventory by the total number of units in the inventory.

That marks the end of this chapter. To practice, why not attempt the fun activity below before proceeding to the next chapter? It could help you tell if you missed out on something in the information provided so far.

Fun Activity

On March 1, 2020, Jennifer purchased inventory worth $1,640 on credit. On that same day, she received a $745 payment for the cash sale of industrial detergents. Prepare journals showing the double entry impact of Jennifer's transactions for the day.

Chapter Summary

- Double entry bookkeeping allows you to post entries to all the accounts that are affected by a transaction.
- Cash basis accounting recognizes only the money that you have received or spent.
- Accrual basis accounting recognizes all the revenue that you have earned and all expenses that you have incurred.

In the next chapter you will learn about the relevance of GAAP to small businesses.

Chapter Two:
Mind the GAAP

Let's switch gears a bit and skip to some discussions about important regulations—the GAAP. These regulations govern financial reporting processes in businesses and other organizations. They might not mean much to your business right now; but you might find them extremely useful in the future.

Take my case for example. I had never given these regulations much consideration until the day a high-flying investor walked out on me because I couldn't provide externally audited financial statements for my business. That's why I felt it wise to share with you the basics of GAAP and where or when it might be needed. I believe it's always good to be in the know to avoid finding yourself clueless in your hour of need, much like I did. So, let's get into this discussion to better understand why I am sharing this with you.

The GAAP is a set of universally applicable rules and regulations that guide the processes of recording, processing, analyzing, and interpreting financial data. All publicly listed companies in the United States are required by law to subscribe to the GAAP. There are 10 core pillars that describe the GAAP-imposed requirements for handling and sharing financial information. The Accounting.com (n.d.) website has summarized these pillars, or principles, as follows.

- Regularity with regards to adherence of accountants to the prescribed regulations.
- Consistency in the application of accounting standards in the entire process of preparing and presenting financial reports.
- Sincerity and commitment to impartial approach on the part of accountants when handling financial information.
- Use of permanent methods to guarantee consistency in the procedural paths taken to prepare financial reports.
- Work ethic that is void of compensation expectations, regardless of the kind of verdict that an accountant expresses about an organization's financial reporting performance.
- Prudential approach to the financial reporting procedures to avoid fomenting speculation.
- Prioritization of continuity in the appraisal of assets with respect to upholding the notion that an organization's operations will remain uninterrupted.
- Observation of periodicity in the scheduling of revenue reporting through consistent use of standard durations like quarters or whole financial years.

- Disclosure of materiality, so that financial reports can provide a clear picture of the prevailing monetary situations of organizations.
- Allegiance to the tenets of utmost good faith by all parties to encourage honesty and transparency.

Origins of the GAAP

In case you are wondering, the GAAP didn't just pop up from thin air. It has been around for a long time and is shaped by both ordinary and historic events. I am always fascinated by the history of the GAAP because past challenges that led to its establishment, such as fraud and embezzlement of funds, are still with us today. I am sure that as your business gradually grows bigger, you will come to appreciate why the GAAP has been around for so long.

The gradual introduction of the GAAP dates back to the early 1930s when efforts began to streamline the reporting procedures of publicly listed companies following lessons drawn from the devastation of the Great Depression. Falsification of accounting data and abuse of financial reporting procedures were some of the major weaknesses that were attributed to the Great Depression. Many companies and corporations collapsed because they manipulated their financial reports to conceal the true picture of their financial health.

The federal government deployed bold responsive measures that began with the enactment, in 1933, of the US Securities Act. This particular piece of legislation was crucial in laying the ground for discussions on further precautionary measures for curbing financial reporting fraud. This led to the enactment of the Securities Exchange Act in 1934, as a more comprehensive legislation for slaying fraud, which was rampant among listed companies. But it wasn't until 1936 that the American Institute of Accountants, using the legal framework provided by the Securities Exchange Act, unveiled the GAAP as binding guidelines for financial reporting and accounting practices.

Although the Securities Exchange Commission (SEC) was the major power behind the legislation that paved the way for the development of the GAAP, it was never involved in the development of the GAAP or the issuance of its pronouncements. This task was left to non-government professional accounting bodies. By 1939, the Accounting Principles Board (APB), in partnership with other accounting bodies, had begun to issue pronouncements that were designed to provide financial reporting guidance for listed companies. These pronouncements formed the foundation of the accounting standards that were established in the years that followed.

In 1973, the Financial Accounting Standards Board (FASB) was established to assume the role of issuing pronouncements of the GAAP, among other functions. FASB still remains in charge of the GAAP today.

Understandably, modifications and improvements that were done on GAAP through the years were not sufficient to curb the financial reporting malpractices. For example, Labaton (2006) reported that the Sarbanes-Oxley Act of 2002 was enacted to protect investors from being swindled by listed companies. Companies kept on collapsing one after another in a chain of events that culminated in the 2008 financial crisis. Companies like Enron, World.com, Toys R Us, Lehman Brothers collapsed due to financial reporting scandals involving jaw-dropping figures.

However, the setbacks that were experienced in past years should be not used to condemn the GAAP as being ineffective. Continuous efforts have been made to seal loopholes that were previously exploited by unscrupulous accountants and managers in corporate organizations. FASB has remained steadfast in providing guidance and ensuring strict adherence to the provisions stipulated by the principles of the GAAP.

The Significance of the GAAP

- The GAAP serves a common reference point for the recommended accounting procedures to ensure consistency of financial reporting across different companies and organizations. This inspires confidence among investors because they do not have to worry about variations that would have been occasioned by different presentations of financial statements of different companies.
- Standardization of the procedures for processing and presenting financial reports makes it easier for stakeholders to interpret and grasp the contents of the reports. It also provides a basis for comparing financial accounts of companies in a similar industry.
- The GAAP is widely perceived as the yardstick of accountability in not only listed companies, but also not for profit and public institutions. The adoption of GAAP in small businesses could also provide a good measure of accountability.

GAAP vs. IFRS

The GAAP is affiliated with many other guidelines and standards that are widely applied to financial reporting. The International Financial Reporting Standards (IFRS) is one such framework that exists side by side with the GAAP. However, just as its name suggests, the IFRS is applied in listed companies that have operations in international locations. It is common to encounter the mention of IFRS in discussions involving the GAAP. But you do not have to bother yourself about the IFRS if your small business operations are not spread to international locations. The IFRS is meant for application by public listed companies with cross-border operations.

Quiz: Would you consider the following statement or true or false? Small businesses are free to choose whether to adopt GAAP or not.
a) False
b) True

Applications in Small Business
Stakeholders in the accounting field have been debating about the relevance of the GAAP to small businesses. The GAAP is by design meant to ensure transparency in the financial reporting processes of companies that have issued stock. The GAAP actually seeks to secure the interests of shareholders and other external stakeholders of publicly listed companies. Moreover, its implementation has significant cost implications that may be burdensome to small

businesses. These are some of the reasons why the question of the relevance of the GAAP to small businesses has always come up.

There have been assumptions that the application of the GAAP in business organizations is the role of professional accountants and accounting firms. However, the truth is that anyone with accounting knowledge should be able to interpret and implement GAAP guidelines. That is the reason this book is imparting this knowledge with you. Once you have the accounting knowledge, you should be capable to do your due diligence to determine your understanding and interpretation of different principles.

To begin with, there is no harm in your small business complying with the GAAP. My bet is that you are running a small business with the hope and ambition of growing into a large business in the future. You may find yourself issuing stocks and facing stricter financial reporting requirements in that journey to growth. Having prior knowledge of the GAAP and its application would be an added advantage to you, should your business undergo this transformation. If anything, some of the so-called large businesses and corporations were all small businesses once upon a time and grew over the years into what they are today.

Planning

Planning is one of the aspects of the GAAP that you will find relevant to your small business. The accrual basis accounting is particularly useful in projecting cash flows trends in your business. This way, you are able to plan depending on the cash inflows and cash outflows you expect to generate over a particular period of time.

Strategic Precaution

You can adopt the GAAP in your business as a precautionary measure to safeguard against fraud in financial reporting. Whereas cost has widely been cited as the major impediment to the adoption of the GAAP in small businesses, you will realize that there is more to lose if your small business is implicated in financial reporting fraud. Lessons from past experience have shown that fraud can be extremely costly to the business in terms of expenses on legal representation, and in extreme cases, the threat of total collapse.

Auditing

There are numerous reasons that will make you want to generate financial reports that are compliant to the requirements stipulated by the GAAP. For example, it is much easier to subject GAAP-compliant financial reports to external auditing. That's because the GAAP prioritizes the interests of external stakeholders, and so does the external auditor. By adopting the GAAP, you would simply be preparing your financial statements from a similar point of view from which an external auditor will scrutinize the reports.

Stakeholder Requirements

The GAAP prioritizes the perceptions and reactions of external stakeholders towards your small business, rather than your individual aspirations. For example, a bank is more likely to perceive your GAAP-compliant financial reports positively compared to non-compliant reports. That should make it easier for you to acquire a loan and build a long lasting partnership with your bank. That's because the lender can estimate with certainty the ability of your small business to generate income to repay a loan, as demonstrated by your income statement and cash flow statement.

For investors, GAAP-compliant financial statements will allow them to determine the fair value of your small business. This is particularly important when investors need to make decisions as to whether or not they should commit their financial resources to your business. This means that compliance with the GAAP gives your financial reports greater credibility that you need to inspire confidence to your external stakeholders.

Taking a Visionary Approach

Incorporating the GAAP in the preparation of financial reports of your small business is absolutely a voluntary decision. Nonetheless, there is always a need to ensure that your subscription to the GAAP is in sync with the mission, objectives, and vision of your small business organization. In other words, your compliance with the GAAP will make sense only if it is relevant to your business operations and strategy. The desire to adopt GAAP guidelines should neither cripple your day-to-day operations nor derail your long-term plans.

The type of your small business and the layout of your growth strategy have direct bearing on the viability of your adoption of the GAAP. If your business is a type that interacts frequently with external stakeholders, then the adoption of the GAAP will be an option worth your consideration. For example, a supplier will scrutinize your business financial profile to be able to tell if you qualify for credit.

You will also find the GAAP extremely relevant if your vision is to grow into a larger organization with greater influence over your target markets. That means any plans to offer shares to the public or supplement the organic growth of your business through merger and acquisition (M&A) deals would make your small business a suitable candidate for adoption of the GAAP. We have already shown that compliance with the GAAP is a mandatory requirement for a company that presents its shares to the public through an initial public offering (IPO) or any other channels of the financial markets.

The issue of an M&A growth strategy is particularly important because federal agencies like the IRS, Federal Trade Commission (FTC) and other regulators will subject your business to intense scrutiny the moment you express interest in purchasing another business. The regulators will look into the various financial and nonfinancial consequences of your acquisition. Antitrust and fair competition issues are also given significant considerations during such evaluations. For example, the FTC, through the Bureau of Competition, will not approve an acquisition that has the potential of transforming your business into a monopoly. The IRS, on its part, will want to probe tax compliance of your business and the business you want to acquire. All these processes will be swift if your business will have achieved GAAP compliance at that particular point.

The issue of cost of implementation and the time you will invest in adoption of the GAAP is a consideration of equal importance. The hiring of accounting professionals and financial lawyers are such cost items associated with the implementation of the GAAP. Therefore, this is one area you will want to be careful to avoid exposing your small business to unbearable financial burden. For example, the accounting knowledge and ability to manage the process on your own will go a long way in eliminating such costs.

Alternatives to the GAAP

Ideas have always been floated about the need to develop alternative principles that are specifically designed for small businesses to avoid the irrelevance and ambiguities associated with the application of the GAAP in such businesses. Numerous organizations have stepped forward with different solutions that are designed to unlock this stalemate. The Association of American Certified Professional Accountants (AICPA) is one such organization that has presented a viable alternative to the GAAP. As of 2020, the AICPA has achieved considerable milestones in developing what it calls the "Financial Reporting Framework for Small- and Medium-Sized Entities."

The FRF for SMEs is a trademarked toolkit of the AICPA, and is meant for use by U.S. small businesses to generate informative, simple, and accurate non-GAAP financial reports. This particular toolkit has been simplified by combining the aspect of cash basis of accounting that is prevalent in small business with the accrual basis accounting. It is actually designed to help small business owners focus on the most relevant aspects of financial reporting.

Like in the previous topic, I have some surprises waiting for you right here! Have some fun sharing your thoughts about the fun activity below.

Fun Activity

The GAAP clearly recommends the use of accrual basis accounting in financial reporting. What is your take about how the matching principle of accrual basis accounting can help you to project your earnings for the accounting period?

Chapter Summary

- The GAAP provides financial reporting guidance and can be used by all types of businesses.
- GAAP adoption is compulsory in listed companies and voluntary in small- and medium-sized businesses.
- GAAP compliance in your small business will make sense only if it is relevant to your business operations and strategy.

In the next chapter you will learn the significance of budgeting and financing in the implementation of your growth strategy.

Chapter Three:
Budgeting and Financing

Going by the way I have framed this topic, does it mean budgeting and financing are twin items? Not really. In fact, they are not the same thing. I have always handled the two as separate disciplines of accounting. But I'll be quick to add that the two are related because they both touch on the funding dynamics in your business.

For example, if you look at it, you will realize that the success of your business strategy and operations depends on the availability of financial resources. As for budgeting, it provides you the opportunity to weigh your income and spending. As such, your financing activities are interwoven with the implementation of your current production activities and future plans. I have discussed both budgeting and financing in greater detail and I know that will help you understand their scope and relevance.

Financing

Savings, retained profits, and personal financial contributions are often cited as the common sources of capital for small businesses. It is always good to prioritize the use of your own funds when seeking startup or working capital to avoid the hurdles of borrowing money from outside sources. However, it is quite unlikely that you will have enough cash at your disposal at all times to fund your business operations. There comes a time when you have to borrow to supplement your own funds.

Consider embracing short term, medium term, or long-term options when seeking sources of finance for your business. It all depends on the profile of the business and urgency of your funding needs. However, never rush into borrowing decisions; give careful considerations to the impact that your preferred source of funding will have on your small business.

The cost of capital should be a priority consideration if you want to avoid paying exorbitant fees for loans. For example, if you borrow a $5,000 short-term loan from a bank, you will expect to pay back the amount at a negotiated fixed interest rate for the duration of the loan repayment. But if you borrow the same amount from an alternative financing source—that is, a source other than a conventional lender—you will pay more in terms of annual percentage rate (APR). APR is an interest rate calculation expressed with reference to a whole year as opposed to monthly calculations.

Let's take a look at a situation where you are repaying the $5,000 at an interest rate of 12 percent per annum; this will result in $600 interest on a one-year loan. For an alternative financing source, such as an online loan, you will be required to repay the $5,000 loan at a specified interest rate within a maximum period of three months. Cumulatively, the APR for the alternative funding will be many times higher compared to the APR of the bank loan. For example, borrowing the $5,000 for a three-month period from an alternative lender at a $600 charge on the principal amount would cost you as follows:

$600 / $5000 = 0.12

= 0.12 x 365 (days in a year) = 43.8

= 43.8 / (30 days x 3 months or term of the loan)

= 43.8 / 90

= 0.4867

Multiply by 100 percent to convert to APR

= 0.4867 x 100

APR = 48.67%

This means that you will incur accumulated interest rate charges of 48.67% in three months in terms of APR. The 48.67% interest rate on the principal loan amount in three months is four times the 12 percent interest you would have paid in a whole year for the same loan from a bank.

Banks are able to charge lower interest rates because they will subject you to rigorous vetting procedures in addition to seeking verifiable guarantors and collateral before giving you a loan. Alternative financing providers will hardly vet you or request for collateral. For example, your digital bank statement will be sufficient to get an online loans provider to determine your maximum loan limit. The high exposure to risk is compensated for through high interest rates they will impose on your loan.

Short Term Finance

Short-term finance is repayable within a period not exceeding one year. It is recommended when you experience deficits in your operating cash flows. Lack of sufficient operating cash flows has the potential of crippling your business operations because you will be unable to pay your bills as they become due. You must find ways of injecting additional funds to your working capital to address the operating cash flow deficits.

The portfolio of short term financing consists of trade credit, bank overdraft, invoice factoring, and alternative financing, among others. Trade credit is an arrangement that allows you to pay for goods or services at a later date as specified by the seller. The seller will offer you a credit period ranging between 7 and 120 days. The duration of the repayment period will depend on the track record of your past credit purchase transactions with the seller and the nature of transaction. An overdraft facility is simply a situation where your bank allows your withdrawal to exceed your account balance. The bank will recover the money plus the applicable fees on your next deposit. You could also borrow a working capital loan from your bank as a short-term fix to shortage of funds in your business.

Invoice factoring involves selling invoices that are not yet due for payment to a third party at discounted prices. The third party will claim the full amounts from your debtors once the invoices become due for payment. Alternative financing includes online loans, merchant cash advances, microloans, and crowdfunding, among others. Providers of alternative financing usually offer very short repayment periods, usually a couple of months, for their loans. As discussed earlier in this chapter the APR cost of alternative loans is higher compared to other types of loans because they do not require security.

Medium Term Finance

Medium term financing provides you with a longer repayment period stretching for up to five years. Hire purchase, lease financing, and bank loans are some of the medium term sources of finance that you may find relevant for your small business. A hire purchase agreement allows you to take possession of an asset after paying an initial deposit. This will be followed by monthly installments that you will pay over a specified duration.

In lease financing, you only take custody rather than own the asset or property in question. A lease agreement allows you to use equipment for a specified duration during which you will pay an agreed sum of money as leasing fees. The entity leasing you the equipment will be responsible for maintenance costs throughout the life of the lease.

A bank loan lasting for more than one year and less than five years is considered a medium term source of finance. You will find this particular source of finance useful when in urgent need of capital for purchasing equipment or machinery for use in your business.

Long-Term Finance

Long-term sources of finance provide you with lengthy repayment periods that could stretch to decades. In some cases, long-term sources of finance usually form part of the capital of your business, especially if it is in the form of equity. In such cases, funds associated with the equity capital will remain at your disposal for as long as your investors retain their shares in your business. You can always transfer the shareholding rights of equity shares through sale to another party whenever an investor elects to quit.

The other viable sources of long-term capital for small businesses include retained profits, venture capital, and term loans. Retained profits are basically portions of your net profit that you put back into the business, while venture capital is a type of private equity that is mostly associated with startup firms. Venture capitalists also provide technical support because they have interest in the long-term growth of the business. But your business must have high growth potential for it to attract venture capital investors.

Long-term loans from banks or other financial institutions are worth considering for investment in projects that require huge capital funding. The advantage of investing borrowed financial resources in long-term investments is that you will use part of the revenues generated by the investments to pay back the loans.

Budgeting

Planning is one of the things that I'm always passionate about. Planning allows me to strike compromises between prevailing realities and future expectations. I always try to find ways of using past and current trends to predict the future performance of my business. My advice to you is that you should try that approach as well because it is based on realistic parameters. There is nothing to gain from not seeing the correct business growth projections.

Speaking of planning, do you prepare a budget at all for your business? And if so, how often do you prepare one? Ideally, you should prepare a budget at least once a year. But there is no harm doing it on a more frequent basis like monthly or quarterly. Don't be the guy who dismisses the need for budgeting just because yours is a small business. There is nothing like small or big business when it comes to planning. How else would you be able to tell the scope of financial resources you need to run your operations efficiently without estimates of your revenue and expenses?

Budgeting Methods

When budgeting for your small business you will most likely be deploying the activity-based, incremental, value proposition, or zero-based method. The activity-based method allows you to match your projected spending on production activities against your ultimate target performance goals. You must first determine your target output for the budget period to be able to estimate the costs that you will incur to be able to deliver on the set goals.

The zero-based method of budgeting entails building your spending projections from scratch. It is a situation where you will be simply saying that your business does not have spending and income projections. Therefore, you get to create your projections all over again as if the business never existed. This way, you should be able to avoid carrying over unnecessary budget items from the previous budgeting period. You will find this particular method of budgeting helpful when seeking to achieve your target output with minimum spending.

The incremental method of budgeting is the simplest option that you should consider when preparing for the budgeting process. It involves the use of the previous year's budget to make spending and revenue projections for the current period. You will be looking at how much more in terms of percentage you need to spend in the current period compared to the previous period to be able to achieve similar or better results. This method of budgeting provides you with flexibility to factor in expanded production activities in your budget. However, the method is likely to present you with challenges if the actual increases in the cost of some production resources exceed your estimations.

The value proposition approach to budgeting is a situation where you prioritize your budget entries on the basis of the productivity credentials of each item. It actually involves a cost-benefit analysis of each of the items you are including in your budget to ensure that you are spending on items whose benefits are in excess of their costs. You will be looking at the contribution that each item will be making towards the achievement of your overall production goals. This is one of the best ways to avoid creating a bloated budget because it helps you avoid irrelevant items.

Quiz: In your opinion, which of the following budgeting methods ties the inclusion of a budget item to its productivity credentials?

a) Activity based method
b) Incremental method
c) Value proposition method
d) Zero based method

Budget Structure
Do you ever find difficulties selecting a budget format? There aren't many choices to begin with. Your choices are limited to either a static or a flexible

budget. If you choose to go with the static method, you will not be able to make any adjustments to your budget regardless of changes in your business environment. The purpose of this limitation is to allow you to prioritize stability and accountability in your business. You just have to learn to cope with unexpected changes that could come your way during the budget period.

As for the flexible budgeting approach, it provides you room to accommodate unforeseen changes in the business environment. You can review your budget to increase or reduce allocations in response to the prevailing circumstances. For example, a sharp decline in your sales would necessitate a downward review of your expenses. Similarly, an unexpected revenue increase could prompt you to review your budget and provide supplementary funding for selected operations.

Types of Budgets
Some of the common types of budgets that you may consider for your business include the sales budget, personnel budget, financial budget, and master budget. You'll generally be looking at the nature and scope of your operations when selecting the most appropriate budget for your business. For example, you should find the master budget useful if you have

multiple departments in your business that generate their own budgets.

Financial Budget

You will find this type of budget useful if you are primarily focusing on revenue and expense projections. The financial budget will also help you set your priorities on the basis of transaction types and spending targets. That's because it summarizes your projected income for the period alongside your planned expenditure on operations and capital investments. The cash budget, operating budget, and capital budget are such financial budgets that you can prepare in your business.

The cash budget allows you to weigh your cash sale estimates against your cash purchases for the accounting period. This way, you can be able to detect any overlaps that may lead to budget deficits. The cash budget is actually anchored on the cash basis accounting where you recognize sales or expenses the moment you receive or pay cash, respectively.

The cash budget should be your perfect choice if you are interested in realistic estimations rather than mere assumptions. It will also help you detect surplus allocations that may leave large amounts of unused cash at the end of the period. However, you will have to come to terms with the gradual transition toward a cashless economy. You may find it difficult to conduct business with entities that do not accept or pay cash.

The operating budget, on the other hand, focuses on the revenue and expenses generated by your routine production activities. This includes revenue from sales and expenses from different functional units within your business.

Capital budget focuses on long-term investments that require large spending. It entails planning for acquisition of fixed assets on the basis of their costs and benefits that they generate over time. You need to consider various long-term investment parameters, such as time value of money, when budgeting for acquisition of capital assets.

Master Budget

The master budget is a bottom-up kind of budget because the process begins from the departments within your business. Each department, be it finance, marketing, IT, or HR, prepares its own budget and forwards it for approval. You may strike out minor items and approve a department's budget or return it with recommendations for amendments if you need to have major items removed. You will then proceed to consolidate the details in the different budgets into a master budget.

The master budget provides you the opportunity to decentralize your planning and involve your employees in decision-making processes. It is also easier to achieve proportional allocation of resources across different departments under a decentralized approach to budgeting.

Sales Budget

When preparing a sales budget, you will be attributing all your revenue and expenses to your sales activities. You will be matching the estimates of your revenue from sales against the estimated expenses that you will incur to achieve the targeted revenue. Your sales budget will feature details such as the types of products, their prices, and unit count of sales forecasts of each product. You also need to list cost items like distribution costs, wages, and commissions, among others. Looking back at the master budget, the sale budget is what you would be expecting from your sales department.

On the flipside, your sales budget could be compromised by issues beyond your control. For example, fluctuations of demand due to changes in economic conditions and growing competition from other players in the market could derail your budget plans. Issues such as sudden changes in government regulations also have the potential of upending your sales activities.

Workforce Budget

You will find this type of budget ideal if you are seeking to focus on your staffing issues. It enables you to estimate your spending on the existing employees and the recruitment of new ones. In a master budget, this relates to the HR department budget. The preparation of a workforce budget as a separate function helps you make accurate projections about your labor requirements relative to the period's production targets.

Budgeting Steps and Procedures

The budget preparation process depends on the budgeting method or type that you are using. However, certain budgeting procedures are universal and you may apply them across board.

- Step One: Create a budget template or download one. Enter the relevant particulars of the budget including your business name, date, and title.
- Step Two: Insert the opening balance carried forward from the budget of the previous period.
- Step Three: Set your estimations of sales and expenses for the budgeting period under review. Past trends or your business plan will be useful in determining your projections of

sales and expenses projections relative to the overall growth trajectory of the business.

- Step Four: List the itemized projections of the cash inflows. This should include a summary of inflows from cash and/or credit sales. Concentrate your efforts toward creating a very clear picture of the projected inflows from all the revenue streams of your small business.
- Step Five: Add the sum of the cash inflows.
- Step Six: List the itemized projections of the cash outflows. This should include a summary of outflows from cash and/or credit purchases. Direct your efforts toward creating a very clear picture of the projected outflows from all the expense outlets of your small business.
- Step Seven: Add the sum of the cash of the cash outflows.
- Step Eight: Subtract the sum of the cash outflow from the cash inflows. A positive figure will be a budget surplus, while a negative figure will be a budget deficit.
- Step Nine: Insert the projected debts, loan repayments, and interest payable in the period. Subtract the loan repayments and interest payable from the total borrowed debts to determine the net amount of cash from your financing activities.

- Step Ten: Add the net figure of financing activities to the budget surplus or deficit to determine the closing balance of the budget.

Well, here is another fun activity for you to attempt. Have fun as you try your luck with it; it's never that serious!

Fun Activity

Arcwyl Agencies closed the budget of the previous period with a $2,500 balance. The company's projected income, expenses, and financial activities are as follows.

First quarter sales – $20,800
Second quarter sales – $31,250
Third quarter sales – $29,320
Fourth quarter sales – $38,420

First quarter cash expenses: raw materials ($9,800), direct labor ($4,500), distribution costs ($2,800), equipment lease ($4,800).

Second quarter cash expenses: raw materials ($12,430), direct labor ($6,100) distribution costs ($3,800) equipment lease ($6,500).

Third quarter cash expenses: raw materials ($11,940), direct labor ($5,820) distribution costs ($3,450) equipment lease ($6,200).

Fourth quarter cash expenses: raw materials ($14,785), direct labor ($7,200) distribution costs ($4,700) equipment lease (4,000).

In the first quarter, Arcwyl Agencies borrowed $4,500 at a 12% interest rate from Bank AZ. The company repaid $1,100 in the second quarter, but borrowed an additional $6,500 at the same interest rate in the third quarter. In the fourth quarter, the company repaid $1,800.

Prepare a cash budget of Arcwyl Agencies showing the projection of the company's income, spending, and financing activities for each of the quarters and for the whole year.

Chapter Summary

- Achievement of your production and growth targets depends on the availability of sufficient financial resources.
- Objective planning involves striking a compromise between prevailing realities and future expectations.
- The budget provides predictive parameters against which you can track and measure the performance of your business.

In the next chapter you will learn about financial statements and their relevance to your small business.

Chapter Four:
Financial Statements

We have finally got to what I consider to be the heartbeat of accounting: financial reporting! This happens to be one of my favorite areas in accounting and I want to make it your favorite too. Whether it's the balance sheet, the income statement, or the cash flows statement, I always find it fun preparing financial reports from the summaries of my financial data. If you also find it fun, there will be never dull moments in your small business accounting.

Still wondering what my excitement with financial reporting is all about? To be honest with you, there are valid reasons behind it. Look at it this way, financial statements—as long as they are not tampered with—provide the most vivid insights into your business activities. I only need a quick glance through your financial statements to tell if your business is headed in the right direction. Information about the growth potential and overall performance of your business is readily available in these statements. It's no wonder financial statements are always among the most sought after sources of information in business organizations!

A word of caution though… This is the one area you need to be careful about, especially with regards to issues that concern truth. Don't entertain the temptation to falsify your financial reports to reduce your tax liabilities or give the wrong impression of your growth prospects. Such misrepresentation of financial information would land you into big trouble with the IRS and other government agencies. Other stakeholders, such as investors and creditors, will shun you as well if they ever get to know that you are not a straightforward person. So many businesses, both large and small, never survive when implicated in financial reporting scandals. Many companies actually collapse! Don't let yours be one of them.

Balance Sheet

The balance sheet summarizes the financial position of your business at a particular date or accounting period. It shows the assets, liabilities, and the capital of the business. When preparing a balance sheet, you need to list the current assets (highly liquid items) and fixed assets (least liquid items. The same applies to liabilities because you need to list the current and long-term liabilities. Capital is basically the equity structure of your business. It shows the amount that you and others have contributed as capital toward the business.

Balance sheet information provides insights into different operational and strategic parameters in your business. For example, the difference between your current assets and current liabilities is essentially the working capital, or short-term liquidity position of your business. This information shows the ability of your business to meet day-to-day financial obligations. Current assets must exceed current liabilities for you to be able to fund your cash operations and settle your bills as they become due. The next chapter provides you with a detailed discussion of working capital.

The balance sheet is also a crucial source of information for anyone seeking the net worth details—that is, the difference between your total assets and total liabilities.

This is based on the balance sheet equation which states that: Assets = Liabilities + Capital (Owners' Equity).

A positive net worth simply means your assets exceed liabilities and your business is on the right path of growth. A situation where liabilities exceed assets should signal a big problem. In fact, that is the reason your small businesses may be declared bankrupt because you owe more than you are owed and you cannot meet your debt obligations.

This shows just how significant the balance sheet is in making internal decisions. You must get your priorities straight in terms of deciding the scope of operations and investments. That is important in determining the scope of financial and production resources that you need to sufficiently fuel those operations and investments. As such, the information contained in the balance sheet allows you to make objective decisions on the basis of the empirical evidence of the prevailing conditions in your business.

The balance sheet also portrays the status of your small business to external stakeholders. Your asset and liability positions relative to the capital you have invested in the business are important indicators of the creditworthiness of your business. A potential lender will use the asset and liability profile of your business as the basis for the decision to give or deny you a loan.

Financial ratios that you can derive from your balance sheet are important indicators of the efficiency of your operations and impact of your investments. You can also use such ratios to determine the overall health of your business. For example, the cash ratio compares readily convertible current assets against current liabilities by dividing cash and equivalents of cash by current liabilities.

Solvency ratio, on the other hand, takes into account cash flows associated with the combined assets and the combined short-term debts and long-term obligations to determine the potential of the business to remain afloat. You can also use the balance sheet information to calculate profitability ratios such as return on investment and profit margin. There are many other ratios that you can calculate from your balance sheet depending on the type of information you want to derive.

Therefore, the balance sheet provides vital information that you need to sustain the growth of your small business. The balance sheet actually provides you the opportunity to showcase the fundamental structure of your small business operations and strategy.

Quiz: Can you guess which of the following entries is not found in a balance sheet?

a) Liabilities
b) Assets
c) Owners' equity
d) Sales

How to Prepare a Balance Sheet

Just like the other financial statements, the beautiful thing about preparing a balance sheet is that you have all the information at your disposal. It is not a complicated process; you only need to have accurate records of your business activities in place.

- Step One: Create a template on a spreadsheet or download one from any appropriate online source
- Step Two: Enter the title of your balance sheet including the name of the business and date.
- Step Three: List your current assets including cash in hand, cash in bank, accounts receivable (credit sales), inventory, and prepaid bills, among others. Add the total of the current assets.
- Step Four: List your fixed assets. This should include items such as land, equipment, vehicles, furniture, and buildings. Calculate the depreciation for the fixed assets. Add the total value of your fixed assets less the depreciation. Find more details about depreciation, or gradual loss of value of fixed assets, in Chapter Seven.
- Step Five: Add the list of your intangible assets with regards to items such as goodwill, copyrights, trademarks, and patents. Calculate amortization for the intangible assets. Get the sum of the intangible asset less the amortization. Find more details about amortization, or gradual loss of value of intangible assets, in Chapter Eight.
- Step Six: Add the totals of all the asset segments together – that is, current, fixed, and intangible assets.

- Step Seven: List your current liabilities. Some of the items that will appear in this section include accounts payable (credit purchases), direct labor costs, postpaid bills, and taxes, among others. Add the total of the current liabilities.
- Step Eight: Add the list of your long-term liabilities including items such as long-term loans and property leases. Get the sum of the total liabilities.
- Step Nine: This is the section where you will add your own capital contribution and partners' contribution if the business is a partnership. Add the capital to retained profits and subtract investments you have made in any government securities. Add the result to the total liabilities to determine the combined total of liabilities and owner's capital. Your balance sheet should end at this point and the total liabilities must be equal to total assets for the balance sheet to be considered accurate.

Sample Balance Sheet of a Small Business

Arcwyl Agencies
Balance Sheet
December 31, 2020

Assets		Liabilities	
Current assets	S	Current libilities	S
Cash in hand	2,240.00	Credit purchases	34,600.00
Cash in bank	6,210.00	Labor	12,600.00
Credit Sales	23,170.00	Postpaid bills	1,800.00
Inventory	29,460.00	Payable taxes	7,150.00
Prepaid bills	930.00	Note outstanding	1,944.00
Total current assets	**62,010.00**		**58,094.00**
Fixed assets		Long term liabilities	
Building	12,000.00	Bank loan	45,930.00
Equipment	63,700.00	Equipment lease	30,930.00
Motor vehicle	20,500.00		
Furniture	4,900.00		
Less depreciation	(11,766.00)		
Total fixed assets	**89,334.00**	**Total long term liabilities**	**76,860.00**
Intangible assets			
Patent	6,100.00	Owners capital contribution	20,000.00
Less amortization	(820.00)	Retained profits	1,670.00
Total intangible assets	**5,280.00**	**Total owners capital**	**21,670.00**
Total assets	**156,624.00**	**Total liabilities**	**156,624.00**

Income Statement

The income statement provides crucial information about the profitability status of your small business. It provides a breakdown of revenue, COGS, gross sales, operations expenses and net profit.

Revenue is simply the sum of sales in a particular accounting period. You could generate sales from a variety of activities including sale of merchandise or services, professional services fees, ticket sales for events, transportation charges, and rental income among others. Interest income from money lent to others also counts towards sales. Revenue trends provide insights into the overall market performance of your products or your business. It is for this reason that revenue is alternatively referred to as the top-line growth indicator of your business.

COGS are the direct costs that you may incur to achieve these sales. These are strictly the material or labor costs that are directly related to the sales. Be careful to not include indirect production costs in your calculation of COGS; you will account for such operating costs at a later stage when calculating the net income. To determine COGS for the period, add the purchases for the period to the beginning inventory and then subtract the closing inventory. Subtract COGS from the total sales to determine your gross sales.

The income statement will show a gross loss if COGS exceeds sales. It will similarly indicate a net loss if the operations expenses exceed the gross sales. That's why the income statement is a crucial source of information about the overall performance of your business.

Analysis of the trends of your revenue and expenses will help you identify areas of weaknesses and strengths in your business. You should be able to detect operations inefficiencies that dented your profit margins for the accounting period. For example, if your accounts payable exceed your collections of accounts receivable, it means that there is a lot that needs to be done to enhance debt collection. Similarly, high inventory costs should signal inefficiencies in the production process. Having access to such information is crucial for enhancing the growth of your small business.

Issues that concern the income or profitability of the business are so important that you should not wait for a whole year to prepare an income statement. It is possible to prepare an income statement more frequently to examine the direction of your business relative to revenue, expenses, gross profit, and net profit. It is always good to detect and eliminate weaknesses early before they inflict extreme damage on your business.

Frequent preparation of an income statement puts you in a better position to track the trends of your business performance. For example, you will want to know the immediate impact of increased investment in inventory on the growth of sales. However, remember that the frequent income statement preparation does not substitute the annual preparation of the report. The annual income statement report provides sufficient samples of data for analyzing the different performance aspects of your business more conclusively.

Income Statement Preparation Approaches

There are two viable approaches to preparing the income statement: the single step approach and the multistep approach. The single step approach is based on the simple formula that states Net Income = Revenues less Expenses.

As such, you would simply add all the revenue sources and subtract the sum of the combined expenses from the result. This is a simple approach that is best suited for use in small businesses like yours. The example below highlights the general structure of the single step approach.

Arcwyl Agencies
Income Statement
December 31, 2020

Revenues	$	Expenses	$
Sales	45,000.00	Cost of goods sold	33,400.00
Proceeds from asset sale	3,500.00	Advertising	3,120.00
Revenue earned from interest	2,800.00	Sales commissions	4,200.00
		Expenses on interest paid	2,680.00
Total revenue	51,300.00	Total expenses	43,400.00
Less total expenses	(43,400.00)		
Net income	7,900.00		

The multistep approach provides greater insights into the inward flow of revenue and outward flow of expenses. This particular approach splits the cost items further to determine the nature of profits or losses that prevail in different stages of your income calculations. For example, the deduction of COGS relates to the gross profits, while the deduction of operating expenses relates to operating profit. This method also helps you determine the pretax profit and the net income. The example below provides deeper insights into this approach.

Arcwyl Agencies
Income Statement
December 31, 2020

Sales		45,000.00
	Cost of goods sold	(33,400.00)
Gross profit/loss		**11,600.00**
Operating Expenses		
	Advertising	(3,120.00)
	Sales commissions	(4,200.00)
Operating profit/loss		**4,280.00**
	Expenses on interest paid	(2,680.00)
Pretax profit/loss		**1,600.00**
	Taxes	(780.00)
Net income from active operations		**820.00**
	Terminated operations	(180.00)
Net income		**640.00**

Net income is alternatively referred to as the bottom-line because it portrays the operational efficiencies of the business. For example, high tax liabilities could drastically reduce your net income in a particular accounting period. But since you do not have control over the federal and state government taxes, you will have to pay those taxes and suffer low profits or even losses. It is for this reason that the federal government offers incentives such as tax credits to help small businesses achieve profitability. Operational expenses like payroll or energy costs are within your control because you can downsize to maintain a lean staff or use energy-saving gadgets to achieve efficiency.

Statement of Cash Flows

Yeah. We are finally there again! Remember Pruitt's riches to rags story in the introduction? I did mention something about how the statement of cash flows would have provided him with a reliable fraud detection mechanism. Now here's a chance for you to understand more about the cash flows statement.

Cash flow is the inward and outward movement of money in your business. The cash flow statement provides detailed summaries of the movement of money during the period under review. The statement of cash flows is split into three main sections comprising operating, investing, and financing activities.

Cash flows from operating activities are attributable to your routine operations, such as cash sales and purchases. Investing activities generate cash flows when you sell or purchase a long-term asset such as equipment. Cash flows from financing activities are associated with the acquisition or repayment of debt. This could be either short-term or long-term debt.

The statement of cash flows plays an important role in the management of your business operations and strategy. For example, it would be difficult for you to track the destination of your incoming funds without the help of the cash flows statement. Your operations could be running smoothly and yet you have misdirected either the funds meant for operations to financing activities or vice versa. Indeed, it would be difficult to detect if you are making losses if you channel the loans you have borrowed to the operations. You are able to detect such errors from the analysis of your cash flow statement.

Just like the income statement, you should prepare the cash flow statement on a frequent basis because it is a very important forecasting tool. Cash flow forecasting involves adding the difference of cash inflow and cash outflow projections to the cash at the beginning of the period. That means your cash flows statement for the current period will play a significant role in forecasting the cash flows for the next reporting period. Cash flow prediction is extremely important in accounting management, to the extent that some businesses prepare cash flows statements on a weekly or monthly basis.

Preparing the Cash Flow Statement

You can prepare your cash flow statements using either the direct or the indirect approach. The direct approach has more to do with cash basis accounting where you recognize only income that you have received or payments you have made. The indirect approach, on the other hand, is anchored on the accrual basis accounting, where you recognize income and expenses regardless of whether or not you have received the cash or paid the outstanding bills. The examples below provide a clear picture of the difference between the two cash flow methods.

Direct Approach

The dynamics of the direct method are such that you will be weighing the actual cash inflows against the actual cash outflows. You will basically focus on income items such as cash sale receipts and income from dividends. For expenses, your focus will be directed on entries like income tax and dividend payments, as well as payroll costs, interest payments and payments for purchases. In other words, the operating cash flows section of the direct method neither takes into account the net income, nor recognizes non-cash items such as accounts receivable and depreciation.

Direct method

Operating activities cash flows

Cash receipts from customers	10,620.00
Cash payments to suppliers	(4,200.00)
compensation of employees	(1,780.00)
Interest payments	(50.00)
Tax payments	(740.00)
Net cash from operating activities	**3,850.00**

Investing activities cash flows

Purchase of machinery	(2,250.00)
Proceeds from sale of furniture	800.00
Net cash from investing activities	**(1,450.00)**

Financing activities cash flows

Long term loan from bank	5,000.00
Payment of interest on loans	(50.00)
Net cash from financing activities	**4,950.00**

Opening cash flow balance	1,100.00
closing cash flow balance	8,450.00

The direct cash flow method is considered to be specific because it provides detailed breakdown of the cash inflows and outflows items. It provides deeper insights into different aspects of your operations. For example, you will find this method useful when you need to go down the specifics about the exact amount of cash spent on various functions or items such as employee payroll and interest payments. According to Boyd et al. (n.d.), these are some of the reasons that

FASB accords this method a lot of credit. However, you have to be prepared to spend more time on the preparation of your cash flow statements when using this method.

Indirect Approach

The indirect approach recognizes the net income dimension of operating activities alongside non-cash items such as accounts receivable and depreciation. You will actually be using the exact net income reflecting in your income statement. Therefore, you have to make appropriate adjustments to account for the impact that non-cash items in the income statement will have on the operating activities. This is where the difference between the direct and indirect method lies. The rest of the entries for cash flows from financing and cash flows from investing activities will remain the same when using either method.

When preparing cash flow statements using the indirect method, you will lift the net income amount right from your income statement and then proceed to perform appropriate adjustments by adding or removing non-cash items. You need to add depreciation back to the net income because it does not involve the actual transfer of cash. The same applies to increase in accounts payable, which is added back because the transfer of cash to suppliers is yet to take place. You will have to add back an increase in inventory and increase in prepaid expenses.

You need to remove accounts receivable from your net income, because the actual transfer of cash from the debtors is yet to take place. You also have to remove gain or loss from sale of assets because of variance between the book value and the actual amount that is paid by the buyer (Boyd, n.d.). Inventory expenses and prepaid income are the other items that you should consider for removal during the net income adjustment process.

Arcwyl Agencies
Statement of Cash Flows
December 31, 2020

Indirect method

Operating activities cash flows

Net income

Add or remove non-cash items		360.00
Depreciation expense	280.00	
Increase in accounts payable	2,500.00	
Increase in accounts receivable	(1,780.00)	
Increase in inventory	2,270.00	
gain in asset sale	(140.00)	
Net cash from operating activities		3,490.00
Investing activities cash flows		
Purchase of machinery	(2,250.00)	
Proceeds from sale of furniture	800.00	
Net cash from investing activities		(1,450.00
Financing activities cash flows		
Long term loan from bank	5,000.00	
Payment of interest on loans	(50.00)	
Net cash from financing activities		4,950.00
Opening cash flow balance		1,100.00
closing cash flow balance		8,450.00

It is now clear that the suitability of either the direct or indirect method of cash flows will squarely depend on your individual priorities, the accounting methods you use, and your objective when preparing financial reports. However, whichever method you choose, always remember that the closing balance in your cash flows statement must tally with the closing balance in the balance sheet cash account.

Taxes & Reporting

For those of us who have been in business for a while now, we know why we sometimes dread the IRS. Personally, I have learned to overcome those fears because I have come to know that all I need is to get my tax reporting right. What should I fear if I have nothing to hide? That is the kind of attitude you should possess at all times. Always ensure that you provide accurate details of every aspect of your tax reporting.

The IRS requires that you report your personal income and any income from any other sources of gainful employment. Whether running a sole proprietorship of partnership business, you must declare in your tax returns all the income associated with your business and other supplementary activities. You will be looking at income from employment, income from trading of shares on the stock exchange, and income from foreign exchange gains among many other sources of income that you may have in addition to your small business.

Therefore, having an income statement in place makes it easier and more convenient for you to report your income in tax returns. It means that you have verifiable information about the income from your small business operations. You do not have to scour through your financial records looking for this information. You will simply lift your small business income data from the income statement and insert it to the respective line items of your tax returns.

Guess what again? I am not done with teasing your mind with my fun exercises. Here's another one for you!

Fun Activity
From what you have read so far, how many segments does a statement of cash flows have? What would be your suggestion about the significance of this segmentation?

Chapter Summary

- The balance sheet summarizes the financial position of your business with reference to assets, liabilities, and capital.
- Trends of revenue and expense fluctuations have a direct impact on the profit for the reporting period of your income statement.
- The statement of the cash flows is instrumental in forecasting future cash inflows and outflows.

In the next chapter you will learn about the different financial analysis and predictive tools for use in your small business.

Chapter Five:
Financial Analysis

Has it ever crossed your mind that the financial data your business generates every day contains a lot of information you can analyze? It's very true and there are so many decisions that you can draw from your analysis! The real motivation behind the in-depth analysis of the financial aspects of your business is that it allows you to base your decisions on proven facts and evidence.

So what does financial analysis entail? It's actually the use of appropriate formulas and tools to evaluate the output and overall health of your business. The ratios that you derive from your analysis portray the prevailing situations in specific segments of your operations, including profitability, budgeting, working capital position, and debt profile. This should help you monitor the impact of your current strategy and make important decisions about future changes or innovations in your small business.

The usefulness of financial analysis goes beyond internal decision-making in your business. Your bankers, investors, and creditors always find these analyses useful as well. A lender does not need all manner of stories about how well your business is doing and how fast you expect it to grow in the next few years. All that the lender will do is scrutinize ratios of important operations parameters of your business. Those digits in the financial ratios are enough to tell the prevailing situation and growth potential of your business. No need for a novel about your business.

Analyzing Your Working Capital

I dread those situations when I am unable to answer questions about my own business. I once found myself in that unfortunate situation when I approached my bank for a short-term loan. It was the first question they asked: So, what is your working capital situation? I found myself mumbling incoherently because I was not prepared for this question. I didn't do my homework well before approaching my bank, and I am sorry to say I never got approved for the loan. So, never stay in the dark about the trends of the capital you've committed to your routine operations.

The banker wanted to know my working capital position because it portrays the short-term liquidity profile of my business. Anyone can be able to tell the state of your operations by simply weighing the sum of your current assets against current liabilities. Current assets comprise cash and items that can be converted into cash within a short period including accounts receivable, stocks, and inventory. Accounts payable, as well as loans, wages, taxes and other expenses that are due for payment within a year are classified as current liabilities. Therefore, the dynamics of working capital management revolve around the day-to-day operations rather than the long-term goals of your business.

Working capital is a very important financial indicator that banks, creditors, and investors use to gauge the overall performance of your business. In addition to measuring liquidity, working capital also reveals the scope of operational efficiencies in your business. Creditors and lenders find such information useful in their decision to do business with you. For example, the working capital position of your business helps your bank determine if you qualify for a loan at all. And if you qualify, your bank will use the information to determine your maximum loan limit and minimum interest rate charges. For a credit supplier, your working capital profile will be useful in deciding your credit limit and maximum repayment period

Current assets must exceed current liabilities for your business to be considered to have sound working capital thresholds. Indeed, you need positive working capital to sufficiently fund ongoing operations but also invest in your growth strategy. But it is advisable to scrutinize the details so that you are not blinded by inflated or misleading figures. In your opinion, for example, would you consider a wide positive working capital margin to be an indication of the sound financial health of your business? You are partially correct if you do, but it's not always the case. This reality should hit home when you think about it in terms of the positive working capital being a consequence of a bloated inventory.

Negative working capital arises when current liabilities exceed current assets. It occurs when the business registers an asset-to-liability ratio of zero and below. This is simply a situation where your business owes more than it is owed. Never entertain negative working capital because it lowers the credit rating of your small business. Operating from the negative zone would raise red flags for any stakeholder that has interests, or is seeking a stake, in your business. For a bank or creditor, it means that your business is not capable of accommodating new debt and paying outstanding debts.

Negative working capital is indicative of inefficiencies in the deployment of assets. Its prevalence is attributable to various factors including bias toward acquisition of long-term investments. For example, if you dedicate too much investment in fixed assets whose benefits are tied to the time value of money, you will not be able to compensate for revenue gaps that will be caused by a shortfall of liquid assets. Such inadequacies may lead to liquidity crises because the business will not be generating enough revenue to offset current liabilities as they become due.

Quiz: Which if the following statements best describes a negative current ratio?

a) A working capital situation where the current assets exceed the current liabilities.
b) The difference between fixed assets and long-term liabilities.
c) A working capital situation where the current liabilities exceed the current assets.

Calculating Your Working Capital Ratio

Since the balance sheet shows the financial position of your business at a particular point, this would be the most ideal source of data for your current assets and liabilities. Take the total figure of current assets in your balance sheet records and divide it by the sum of current liabilities to get your working capital ratio. In the absence of a balance sheet, you will have to derive your data from your general ledger.

- Step One: Create a four-column Excel worksheet template. Label the first, the second, the third, and the fourth columns as current liabilities, amount, current assets, and amount, respectively. This means that you will have your current liabilities on the left side of the template and the current liabilities on the right side.

- Step Two: List all the current liabilities and their respective amounts as captured in the general ledger. Add the sum of the figures in the amounts column and insert it at the bottom of the column.
- Step Three: List all the current assets and their respective amounts as captured in the general ledger. Add the sum of the figures in the amounts column and insert it at the bottom of the column.
- Step Four: Skip one cell under the total amount in the column for current assets and copy paste the total amount in the current liabilities column. Divide the total current assets by the total current liabilities amount to get the current ratio of your working capital.

The use of an Excel template is just one of the several approaches that you can use to calculate your working capital. The Excel worksheet makes it easier for you to keep records of your working capital calculations. It also provides you the convenience and consistency because you can reuse your template in future calculations. But feel free to use any other preferred approach if you are not used to or comfortable with Excel worksheets. For example, you can simply use a calculator to get the sum of current assets and divide it by the sum of current liabilities.

Analyzing Your Personnel Expenses

This is the one area you don't want to mess with. Getting your employee expenses wrong spells big trouble. You really don't want to have an angry workforce or a slowdown in your business because of high turnover!

That's why you must always prioritize the timely payment of employee salaries and wages. But this being an expense, it is advisable that you take extra measures to evaluate the impact of the personnel costs. That's because personnel costs stretch beyond the direct expenses on salaries and wages to include indirect expenses as well.

Direct expenses consist of spending on employee remuneration items like gross salary, allowances, statutory deductions, benefits, and bonuses, among others. There are occasions where you may provide extra facilities, such as smartphones and laptops. You may also incur rental and utility costs as well as office supplies expenses to ensure that your employees are well-equipped to perform their duties. All these extra costs that you incur other than the direct expenses are indirect expenses. The combination of the direct and indirect expenses is what constitutes the total cost of your employees. Karpe (2018) observed that the personnel cost is the relationship between the annual gross income and annual total cost of the employees.

Yours being a small business, it is unlikely that you will be able to offer your staff all the packages associated with employment. The scope of personnel expenses is quite broad; it would require a conglomerate with considerable financial muscle to absorb high employee costs. For a small business, it will be ideal to provide terms of employment that your business can afford. That means offering some of the nonessential salary items selectively and exploring alternatives like freelancing and remote working arrangements. That's the reason you need to deploy appropriate tools to monitor the total cost of your personnel.

Personnel expenses analysis is meant to help you determine the total cost of your employees relative to other costs in your business. There is no shortage of analytical tools or approaches you can use to achieve your objective of determining the scope of your employee costs. One of these approaches involves analyzing the personnel cost of each individual employee, and then getting the sum of the cost of all employees.

The factor of the annual personnel cost of each employee will be annual total cost/annual gross income. Let's assume your employee has an annual gross salary of $24,000 and annual total cost of $30,000, the factor of the annual personnel cost for this particular employee will be $30,000/$24000 = 1.25. Therefore, to get the personnel cost for each of the remaining employees, you will simply multiply their gross income by 1.25.

Analyzing Your Profits

Profitability analysis entails examining the income output that is attributable to the different investments that you have channeled into the business. Return on assets (ROA) and return in invested capital (ROIC) are some of the common ratios that you can use to measure profitability or earnings.

ROA portrays the portion of the net income that is attributable to the combined value of your assets. To calculate the ROA of your small business, divide the net income by the total value of your assets. Use the net income and value of total assets that you have captured in your income statement and balance sheet, respectively.

ROA actually compares the net income from your active operations against the total value of the assets that contributed toward the income generation. There are various analytical perspectives that you can focus on here, including the intensity of asset use relative to the unit value of profit generated by the assets.

Whereas low-value assets will generate higher profit for each dollar invested, high-value assets will comparatively generate lower profit per dollar investment. That is because the higher the valuation of an asset the higher the impact of its cost implications on the income. This means that a business that has invested heavily on equipment will have a lower profit per dollar investment because of the high spending that was incurred to acquire the assets. Returns associated with such assets will be spread over a longer duration.

ROIC, on the other hand, weighs the profits you have earned against the actual amount of money you contributed to the business. In a listed company, this will include all sources of capital including the bearers of equity and bonds. The ROIC and return on equity (ROE) are designed for use in listed companies.

What is Debt Ratio?
Debt management should always rank among your operations and strategic priorities. The level of

debt in your business affects different other parameters of your financial management objectives. The more you borrow, the more you expose yourself to the risks of filing for bankruptcy due to the inability to pay creditors and lenders. In other words, there should always be a balance between the amount of debt you owe, the amount that you are owed, and the capacity of the business to repay existing debts.

Debt ratio provides comparison between the total money you owe against the total value of your assets. This is the ratio that you, or any other interested party, will be scrutinizing when determining the ability of your business to repay outstanding debt. You can also use the ratio to gauge whether or not your business is capable of accommodating additional debt. This way, you can tell the percentage of debt that you spent on the acquisition of your assets.

To calculate your debt ratio, divide the amount of your total debt by the total value of your assets. These details are readily available in your balance sheet. Your business should have a low debt ratio for it to be considered stable and promising. A ratio of less than one is the recommended level of your debt-to-asset profile. Such a low ratio means that your assets exceed liabilities.

Am I done trying to engage your interest through my quizzes? Nope! Not yet. Here's another one that I want you to crack for me. Keep it simple as usual!

Fun Activity

Using the details in the sample balance sheet in Chapter Four, calculate the working capital of your small business. Based on the outcome of your calculation, what would you comment about the level of working capital for this particular business?

Chapter Summary

- The working capital current ratio highlights the liquidity position—that is, the ability of your small business to pay short-term debts.
- Earnings ratios like ROA and ROIC are useful in measuring the profit trends of your business.
- Debt ratio allows you to monitor the level of debt relative to the total value of assets in your business.

In the next chapter you will learn to deploy accounting software and automation tools for your small business.

Chapter Six:
Software Assistance

In this era of digitization, it has become impossible to speak about accounting without the mention of software tools. There is always excitement when new apps and other digital solutions hit the scene. App innovators are similarly busy trying to outdo each other as they seek to build apps that can automate various financial reporting and other accounting functions.

I am sure you'll agree with me that there is a lot of automation taking place in businesses. Apps and websites have almost become must-haves for any business. Although I'm of the opinion that accounting software is not a new phenomenon, I always acknowledge the immense potential of new and emerging software solutions.

Accounting software has the potential of transforming your routine business operations. You will find it easier to manage the flow and processing of financial data and trace transaction entries to particular individuals. This increases accountability, because erroneous or fraudulent entries can be traced to particular individuals within your team. It actually becomes easier for you to fix pilferage issues when you have such software automation in place. You will also enjoy the convenience of managing your inventory because you can always access the real time data of sales and the remaining items in your stores or shelves at any particular time.

The total cost of ownership will be one of the priority areas of concern when seeking to install an accounting software system. This is an issue that you can always address through the use of an appropriate strategy that is designed to offset benefits against costs. And if you find it extremely costly to automate your entire accounting function, you have the flexibility of selectively automating certain critical functions. For example, you can choose to automate the payroll, revenue collection, payments, or any other function that is a priority to you. This is done through the use of modules that are designed for those particular functions.

Selecting a Tool

When selecting accounting software, you should be guided by the essential features that your preferred tool will provide. You need to ask yourself very important questions about the viability of each particular software tool. Basically, you should be asking three questions:

- Does the software tool have user friendly features?

- Is it flexible to customization?
- What reporting functionality features does it have?

A robust software assistance platform should be able to generate key performance indicators for your business. You should be able to access billing details, profit trends, and tax payment summaries with a click of the mouse. Tasks such as budgeting and planning should become easier with the automation mechanisms of the software platform.

Weigh in the options of deploying a fee-based service from a software vendor instead of acquiring your own accounting software system. A software vendor generally hosts the operating infrastructure and provides the training required to use an accounting system. You will have all the access rights required to feed, process, and manipulate financial data as well as to generate financial reports. Your software service provider will in turn charge you monthly fees. This could be a viable option if it turns out to be cheaper than the total cost of ownership involved in installing your own accounting system.

There is also the option of subscribing to online accounting tools. You can access these tools through websites or apps of the software providers. Some of these tools are available for free, while others charge for either registration or monthly subscription fees. It is important to scrutinize the scope and quality of the services offered by free online accounting software tools. Some of them do not guarantee the safety of their systems and this could leave your data vulnerable to hackers and other online security threats.

Common Tools for Small Businesses

I love free things, and I know I am not alone! I will try free software solutions before spending a single penny on paid solutions. I always consider myself lucky whenever free software works for me. I'll actually do my best to get the most out of it. Unfortunately, truly viable free software tools are becoming scarce by the day. I am now trying my best to get used to software offers that provide a month-long free trial.

What about you? Hopefully you don't share my obsession for free stuff. There is no harm using a free software tool, as long it serves the purpose. If you are interested in free accounting software tools, then you may consider signing up for Akaunting, CloudBooks, Wave, and Zipbooks, among others.

But never hesitate to spend money on paid tools because they come with extra features that are not available in free tools. According to Yakal (2020) some of these paid tools that are worth the money include FreshBooks, GoDaddy Bookkeeping, Intuit QuickBooks Online, Kashoo, Sage 50cloud, Xero, and Zoho Books.

Most of these tools actually have functionalities that make it easier for you to perform your billing and invoicing tasks. Just imagine a situation where you have all the data and profiles of your customers and suppliers in one place. If you need to send out an invoice for a credit sale, all you need to do is to take a photo of the document with your Smartphone and upload it to the app of the software tool. This sets in motion a series of procedures that will link the particulars in the document to the respective account of the debtor. Such particular include the date of the invoice, name of business, address, location, amount, and due date of payment. The same procedure applies for your credit purchase invoices.

The functionality features of these tools are not restricted to the management of your credit sales and credit purchases. They actually provide features that are designed for use in your entire ecosystem of business transactions including cash sales, banking, and financial reporting.

Each of these accounting tools has unique features that may prompt you to choose one over the other depending on your order of priorities. For example,

Intuit QuickBooks Online has often been cited for providing a user-friendly interface and robust data processing features. The Intuit QuickBooks Online affords you the privilege of capturing and processing your business transactions from remote locations. This particular tool has the capabilities of reading the particulars on a picture of a receipt or purchase order and transferring the details to the respective forms. In other words, you simply take a photo of your receipt or purchase order and the software tool will perform the rest of the tasks involved in transferring the particulars to the destination records.

Yakal (2020) identified ZohoBooks and Xero as some of the tools that allow you to create virtual documentation for sales and purchases in addition to supplementary documents like credit notes and debit notes. This is made possible by templates that come as built-in features in these particular accounting software tools. Such convenience makes it easier for you to track your payments and receipts. Some of these software tools actually provide capabilities for tracking your transactions in real time.

Quiz: In your estimation, which of the following is not a software tool for small business accounting?

a) GoDaddy Bookkeeping
b) Intuit QuickBooks Online

c) Zoho Books
d) Xerox Machines

Considerations in Setup

The adoption of software automation tools in accounting is a systematic process that requires proper planning. Your setup considerations should take a variety of factors into account, including the number of people that will be using the system, account access rights and limitations for each user, and overall maintenance of the system. Ordinarily, the level of access will depend on the hierarchy within your business, with your senior employees getting unrestricted access as compared to limited access for the junior ones.

The duration and complexity of the setup process depends on the volume of your financial data and some of the preliminary procedures that you need to perform. For example, you may have to adjust the settings of the software platform to customize it to your individual preferences. This procedure is important because each business is unique and there are certain aspects of the system that you must adjust to accommodate your business profile.

Proceed to fill out your personal and business profiles. Although the required profile details may vary across different systems, you will ideally be filling out information such as business name, contact details, physical address, tax identification number, type of business, and your financial year, among others. It is also at this point that you are likely to be asked to specify the target number of users and your desired features. Such information will be important for the provider to determine the appropriate plan for your business. You will definitely pay more for a higher number of users and sophisticated features. Take a conservative approach to limit the number of users and features to minimize costs.

Some types of software accounting tools will require you to integrate your online payments and merchant platforms such as debit/credit cards or PayPal. Such platforms will be useful in settling your bills with the software provider, but also in integrating capabilities for online sale and purchase transactions. Such integrations work particularly well in the management of accounting software for accounts payable or accounts receivable.

Feed all the relevant data categories that will be required to facilitate transaction processing and financial report generation. This will be essentially a record of your products and/or services, alongside information such as pricing and packaging. You will definitely have more volume of data to feed into the software system if your business has been around for a while. This is because it is generally recommended that you keep data dating back to at least three years for tax filing purposes. The IRS goes back three years, or even longer, when analyzing and comparing your tax filings against your financial statements. Therefore, it is worth your effort to key in all your active or relevant data in, instead of having some of it scattered in your previous physical records.

Employee details will be required if your system has incorporated the payroll processing feature. This is one area you should be prepared to spend a bit of time on because of the intricate nature of payroll processing. You will also have to factor in entries for income tax, tax deductions, and tax relief calculations for your employees. However, do not perceive this as a complicated process. The software assistance system is programmed to generate automated calculations the moment you put in data. Your main task is to ensure that you are providing accurate data.

For your accounting system to be complete, you need to feed that data associated with all the external stakeholders that the business interacts with. This includes customers, suppliers, and government agencies. For example, your employee details must conform to their IRS profiles for your system to process the payroll accurately. Customer and supplier details are important for billing and invoicing.

Best Practices

There are recommended best practices for adopting software accounting systems in your business. Although these practices are not compulsory, they could help you overcome certain hiccups that could derail the achievement of your objectives. In fact, you could find yourself abandoning your accounting software assistance systems due to lack of a clear implementation plan. This would be unfortunate because you will have nothing to show for the time and initial financial investment that you committed to the software program.

Piloting involves adopting a new accounting software system in limited scale to evaluate its viability to your business operations. You should always start with piloting the accounting software to test the scope and limitations of its functionality features. This is the point where you can witness the efficiencies that the system will generate and make a decision on whether or not to proceed with it. Piloting helps you make software adoption decisions well in advance to avoid wasting resources in a system that may not be viable for your business.

Your satisfaction with the relevance of any particular accounting software sets the stage for its full scale installation and widespread use. Ensure that you work closely with the provider of the software tool, or follow the provider's installation instructions, to quickly get your system up and running.

You should then proceed to the training phase to bring your employees on board. All the people using the system must be knowledgeable of its functionalities to be able to perform their respective tasks. You should approach training as a continuous process rather than a one-off affair. That is because the dynamic nature of software platforms due to frequent upgrades and new features that are introduced by providers.

Always remember that adoption of software assistance is not always a smooth ride, especially when dealing with employees that fear being made redundant by the system. It is true that there are occasions when a software system can automate all the functions that were being performed by certain employees. In such situations, you will have to either reassign such employees to different roles or terminate them altogether. This is sometimes the unfortunate end result of the system.

Leveraging Reporting and Help
Just like other automated software systems, accounting tools often provide technical help channels. These include support centers, email addresses, or hotline numbers listed on the provider's

website. You will always find these channels useful whenever you encounter technical problems with installation, software upgrades, data processing, or information output errors.

Support centers or chat portals should be your first stop when seeking help for technical setbacks or functional hitches on your accounting platform. These channels provide access to instant solutions to your problem whenever possible. There are also software platforms that provide a help center where you can find solutions to common problems. This makes it possible for you to attempt to resolve a problem by yourself before contacting your software provider. Online communities are also useful channels for resolving technical issues.

Advantages of Small Business Automation Tools

Having software tools in place puts you in a better position to interact with the transaction platforms of other businesses. The other advantages of accounting tools include:

- Ease of storage of financial data.
- Elimination of repetitive tasks from routine operations of the business.

- Convenience of evaluating the output and performance of individual employees and teams within the business.
- Ability to gather data about trends in your business operations.
- Profit growth due to cost savings associated with maintaining lean operations.
- Accuracy in processing financial data and generating reports.

Disadvantages of Small Business Automation Tools

The introduction of accounting software tools could spell doom for your small business if you do not embrace some degree of caution in your implementation procedure. For example, you could affect staff morale if you do not involve your employees in the process. Fears of job losses among employees could also spark resistance to change or outright sabotage of the system by employees in some cases. The initial cost of acquisition and maintenance costs for paid tools, as seen earlier in this topic, is always a source of concern for small businesses. Costly automation systems for business accounting will increase your investment and operations costs, and subsequently compromise your profit margins.

Well, you can now begin the countdown. Three more fun activities to go! But, as usual, let's wrap this chapter up with a fun question for you!

Fun Activity

The proliferation of free accounting software tools has made it easier for a small business like yours to adopt these tools for day-to-day operations. Why would you prioritize free software over paid software systems for your small business?

Chapter Summary

- Automation of financial reporting processes is a strategic decision with benefits that are realized over time.
- There are various options for adopting accounting software assistance, including acquisition of a platform, use of vendor-managed systems, and subscription to online accounting tools.
- Always follow the recommended best practices when adopting software accounting systems in your business.

In the next chapter you will learn how to calculate depreciation when performing the valuation of your fixed assets.

Chapter Seven:
Depreciation

Having been an expert in accounting and finance for many years, I have encountered many small businesses owners seeking taxation advice. And it has become a common trend for me to come across folk that have no idea about the need to account for loss of value of properties in their businesses. I mean, some business owners had no idea of the taxation benefits they stand to reap from it! I hope you are not one of them. But if you are, don't worry. It's my pleasure to help you learn and understand why it matters.

Depreciation occurs when your tangible fixed assets lose value over time. Such assets include automobiles, computers, buildings, equipment, furniture, and printers. Land does not form part of these assets because it appreciates in value over time.

So, where does the issue of taxation come in? Okay, let's look at it this way. Depreciation is an expense because it chips away at the value of your assets. This means that the valuations of your assets in the balance sheet keep diminishing every year. It is for this reason that the IRS requires to account for the depreciation amount of each year as a deductible item in your Form 4562 tax return filings.

Depreciation mainly affects the fixed assets of your business because it must be spread over the duration of an asset's existence. The IRS-recommended thresholds for determining an asset that can be depreciated include ownership, predictable useful life, multiyear lifespan, and deployment in your business.

Ownership simply means that an asset must be a property of your business for you to be able to subject it to depreciation. As such, you cannot include leased or borrowed assets in your depreciation schedule. The issue of predictable useful life is important because depreciation is only applied to assets that generate value for the business. Useful life lasts between the point you purchase an asset and the point it hits its residual value—that is, the price at which you can sell the asset once it exhausts its usefulness. The determination of the useful life of an asset is not an arbitrary decision; it calls for careful considerations of different parameters that have a bearing on the economic characteristics of the asset. Alternatively, refer to the IRS tax code to access the recommended productive life spans of different assets.

A multiyear life span requirement simply restricts depreciation to your fixed assets. In other words, you cannot depreciate your inventory and other current assets because they have a lifespan of less than one year. As for the requirement that a depreciated asset must be part of your business, it concerns the asset's contribution to the overall productivity of the business. For example, if you purchased a lawnmower for your landscaping business but restricted its use to your home, it would not qualify for depreciation.

How to Keep Track of Depreciation

Wondering how you can keep track of the depreciation of assets in your business? Consider creating a depreciation schedule to keep track of the annual valuation of all your fixed assets. This particular schedule will help you monitor overlaps in the useful life durations of different assets in addition to allocating accurate annual depreciable amounts to the assets. Create a table providing summaries of the particulars of each asset and the depreciation parameters that you are applying on each asset. Such particular include description, purchase price and date, productive lifespan, current valuation, expected residual value, and applicable depreciation method.

How to Account for Depreciation

Since depreciation is an expense item, you should record it both in the income statement and in the balance sheet. In the income statement, you will post the amount under the depreciation expense account. As for the balance sheet, the accumulated depreciation account will be the destination for posting this expense. To capture this transaction in your journal, post a debit entry of the amount in the depreciation expense account and a credit entry of the same amount to the accumulated depreciation account.

Account	Debit	Credit
Depreciation Expense	$1,257.60	
Accumulated Depreciation		$1,257.60

The double above entry simply means that your depreciation expense has increased, while the value of accumulated depreciation has increased by a similar margin. When you transfer the amount to the income statement, the depreciation expense will reduce your revenue for the accounting period. And since the asset has set value, you must capture that change as well in the respective account of that particular asset. This requires making a contra entry—that is, a reversing entry on the opposite side of an account, of the amount you posted in the accumulated depreciation account. In other words, since you have credited the amount in the accumulated depreciation account, you will debit the same amount in the respective asset account.

Quiz: Now that I mentioned a contra entry in the discussion already, how would you define it?

a) An entry that reverses the amount of money in a destination account.
b) An entry that increases the amount of money in a destination account.

What are the Applicable Methods for Depreciation?

When it comes to calculating the depreciation of your fixed assets, you must select a relevant depreciation method from a list of options that include the straight-line, the double-declining balance, the units of production, and the sum-of-the-year's-digits. Your choice of a method should be guided by the impact it will have on your accounts relative to historical cost, deployment, useful life, and salvage value. Let's first look at the different types of depreciation methods and then explore the impact or consequences of each method later on.

Remember that once you choose a depreciation method, you have to stick to it throughout your financial reporting for consistency. You cannot change your method of depreciating your assets midway an accounting period or financial year. And if you are to change the method at all, then you must seek the approval of the IRS. According to the IRS (2020) you will have to "file Form 3115, Application for Change in Accounting Method, to request a change in your method of accounting for depreciation." This shows just how important it is to be sure of the depreciation method you want to use before committing yourself to any particular choice.

Straight-Line Method

The straight-line depreciation should be your obvious choice if you are seeking a smooth ride in your depreciation calculations. It is the simplest method you can think of because it apportions depreciation in equal installments throughout an asset's productive life. To calculate depreciation, subtract the projected residual value from the historical (purchase) cost of the asset and divide the result by the useful life (IRS Tax Code-referenced) of the asset.

To understand the formula for the straight-line depreciation method more clearly, let's use hypothetical figures to look at a practical example. Let us assume you spent $1,000 to acquire a laptop computer that has $150 residual value and a useful life of five years. Your depreciation calculation will be ($1,000 - $150) / 5 = $170. This means you will be allocating $170 as the depreciation amount over the five years of your laptop's useful life. If you want to post the accounting entries, you will post $170 as a debit entry in the income statement and post the same amount as a credit entry in the accumulated depreciation account. You will then proceed to post the same amount as contra entry of the laptop computer account in the accumulated depreciation account.

What happens if an asset use does not last a full year? This is a common occurrence because of the difference in time between the date of purchase and the end of your financial year. In such situations, the IRS requires that you restrict your depreciation calculations to the months that the asset was in use. For example, if you purchased the laptop five months into your financial year, you will prorate your depreciation calculation for the first year to the seven months of use. Therefore, the first year depreciation of your laptop will be $176 x 7/12 = $103.

This shows just how easy and convenient it is to use the straight-line depreciation method. That's the reason this particular method is widely used by small businesses in financial reporting. But that does not mean the other methods are irrelevant. It is worth looking at the other depreciation methods and weighing each one of them against the particular asset you need to depreciate before selecting your preferred method. Each of the depreciation methods has its own advantages and disadvantages as we are going to see later in this chapter.

Double-Declining Balance Method

The double-declining balance method of depreciation will be a convenient choice if your primary motivation is to recover the value of your asset in advance. That is because the method allows you to deduct high amounts of depreciation from the original value of the asset in the initial years, followed by lower amounts in the latter years.

When using this method, your first-year deduction will be double the amount that you would have deducted from the historical cost when using the straight-line method. In the subsequent years, you will be using the book value – that is, the historical cost less the previous depreciation charge. By so doing, you would be diminishing your revenue and asset valuation by higher margins during the application of the initial depreciation charges on the asset. But you stand to reap bigger rewards in the latter years when the depreciation charges dip to low amounts.

Doubling of the straight-line method involves the rate of depreciation rather than the actual depreciation amount. Therefore, you have to calculate the depreciation rate of the straight-line method by dividing 100 percent by the number of useful years. Multiply the result by 2, and then multiply the second result by the historical cost of the asset to determine the depreciation for the first year. If we were to go back to our example for calculating the depreciation of a laptop using the straight-line method, our depreciation rate will be 100/5 = 20. Therefore, the first year depreciation of the laptop under the double-declining balance method will be 20/100 x 2 x $1,000 = $400. This means you will write off $400 from the historical cost of the asset in the first year to leave a book value of $600.

The same formula will apply in your calculation for the depreciation for the second year, only that you will be using the book value instead of the historical cost. For our example above, this will be 20/100 x 2 x $600 = $240. This will leave you with a book value of $360 for the calculation of depreciation of the third year, which will actually dip to $144. For this particular asset, you will have to halt the depreciation calculations in the fourth year because the book value of the laptop will have reduced to $129.60 and its residual value is $120. But you have to post the remaining $9.60 to the depreciation expense account and the respective asset account to reduce the asset's valuation to the exact residual value.

Unlike other depreciation methods, residual value does not feature in your calculations when using the double-declining balance method. Instead, you will keep using the book value until the point when it drops to the same level as the residual value. So what happens when you reach the residual value before the end of the IRS-recommended useful life? Well, there is no problem with stopping earlier because you will have done your bit accounting for the depreciation of your asset relative to its historical cost and book values. In fact, the IRS recommends that the depreciation calculation should end the moment you complete the recovery process of your cost or when you stop using the asset due to exhaustion of its economic value. But you will have to indicate the adjustment of the useful life of the asset in your amended returns, according to the IRS (2020).

The example above shows that the double-declining balance method is essentially an accelerated approach of accounting for depreciation. The important point to remember here is that the depreciation calculations from the second year onwards are based on the reducing balance of the value of the asset. Take note that there are no guarantees of the diminishing depreciation charge translating into benefits. Those benefits could be wiped out by high repair and maintenance costs of an asset. Such would be the case if the asset in question is a vehicle.

Units of Production Method
The units of production method should be your ultimate choice if you want to tie depreciation to the

output trends of your fixed assets. This particular method actually allocates the depreciation cost according to the expected total output of an asset during its useful life relative to the asset's production output for the accounting period under review. This means you must calculate both the depreciation expense of each unit and the total depreciation expense for the entire accounting period.

Let's look at another example to understand how this particular depreciation method works. Assume that the milk packaging equipment you purchased for $90,000 has a residual value of $30,000, a useful life of 1 year, and is capable of producing 100,000 units over its useful life. The packaging equipment produced 1,200 units in the current accounting period. Use the units of production method to calculate the equipment's depreciation for the accounting period.

Begin by subtracting the asset's estimated residual value from its historical cost, then divide the result by the total number of units that the asset will produce during its useful life. This will give you the depreciation of each unit item. For the example above, per unit cost of depreciation will be $90,000 - $20,000 / 100,000 = $0.7. Multiply the depreciation cost per unit by the number of units produced in the accounting period as follows: $0.7 x 1,200 = $840. This is the amount that you will post as the depreciation expense of the milk packaging equipment for the current accounting period. The accounting entries will increase your depreciation expense by $840 and decrease the valuation of the milk packaging equipment by $840.

The depreciation cost for the accounting period will increase with an increase in volume output, and vice versa. For example, if the number of units produced in the current accounting period increases to 1,500, then the total depreciation expense for the period will be $0.7 x 1,500 = $1,050. As such, the more active an asset, the higher the depreciation expense attributable to it, and vice versa. In other words, you do not want to have machinery or equipment that produces insufficient numbers of units or stays idle throughout the accounting period. Such idle fixed assets will deny you the opportunity to claim depreciation expense when filing your tax returns.

Generally, an equipment or machinery will produce more units when still new and fall in output over time due to aging, repairs and maintenance. Adopting the units of production method allows you to determine if you're making the most of your equipment and machinery when they are still new. You stand to reap more benefits over time if you are able to allocate a higher depreciation expense during the initial years of the useful life of your equipment.

Application of the units of production is best suited for your production line machinery or equipment. You will find the method useful in your small business if you want to quantify the output of your assets and allocate the depreciation expense according to the activity levels of each asset. However, the use of this particular method requires close tracking of the output of each equipment or machinery in your production line. You must be able to track both the hours that an asset is in service and its volume of output. This can be quite a tasking exercise if the equipment in question does not have built-in activity tracking features.

Sum-of-the-Year's-Digits Method
The sum-of-the-year's-digits method is based on the principle of recovering the cost of an asset in the early years of its useful life. Its calculation begins with adding together all the digits that constitute the useful life of your fixed asset. For example, if your fixed asset has a useful life of 7 years, the calculation will be $1 + 2 + 3 + 4 + 5 + 6 + 7 = 28$. This will allow you to derive a year-by-year fraction for determining the rate of depreciation. For example, your depreciation rate for the first year will be $7/28 = 1/4$, while the

depreciation rate for the second year will be 6/28 = 3/14, and so on.

Now, for you to determine the depreciation for each of the years, you multiply the rate of depreciation of a particular year by the book value of the fixed asset for that year. Therefore, the first year depreciation will be the purchase price less the salvage value multiplied by that year's depreciation rate. The second year depreciation will be the purchase price less the sum of the depreciation of the first year and the salvage value, multiplied by that year's depreciation rate. For example, let's use hypothetical figures of $24,000 purchase price, $8,000 salvage value, and six-year useful life for your small business pickup truck. The depreciation of the pickup truck will be as follows.

Total of the digits of the useful life: $1 + 2 + 3 + 4 + 5 + 6 = 21$
Rate of depreciation in year one: $6/21 = 2/7$
Depreciation in year one: ($24,000 − $8,000) x $2/7$ = $4,571.43

Rate of depreciation in year two: $5/21$
Depreciation in year two: ($20,000 - $8,000) x $5/21$ = $3,809.52

Rate of depreciation in year three: $4/21$
Depreciation in year three: ($20,000 - $8,000) x $4/21$ = $3,047.62

Depreciation rate in year four: $3/21 = 1/7$
Depreciation in year four: ($20,000 - $8,000) x $1/7$ = $2,285.74

Depreciation rate in year five: $2/21$
Depreciation in year five: ($20,000 - $8,000) x $2/21$ = $1,523.80

Depreciation rate in year six: $1/21$
Depreciation in year six: ($20,000 - $8,000) x $1/21$ = $761.90

We have purposely calculated the depreciation for all the six years to demonstrate the scope difference between the annual depreciation expense of the initial years and those of the latter years. You will find this method useful if you prefer to allocate much of depreciation expense when the asset is still new, and attracting less maintenance and repair costs.

The Modified Accelerated Cost Recovery System (MACRS) Method

The MACRS is a method that allows you to make annual deductions for the depreciation of your fixed assets using IRS-recommended useful life spans. This method is specifically used for taxation purposes, especially for filing claims for depreciation expenses in tax returns (Warnes, 2020). MACRS classifies assets into different categories that specify the useful life of each type of asset. For example, if you want to determine the depreciation characteristics of a lawn mower in your landscaping business, MACRS specifies for you the asset category and useful life duration of that particular asset. The IRS provides a detailed breakdown of the MACRS depreciation table. According to Warnes (2020) you can access these details in Appendix B of Publication Number 946 of the IRS.

However, as Warnes (2020) observed, this particular method is quite complicated and it is advisable to stick to the simpler methods that you have learned already. The MACRS approach is better left to your hired financial experts or, where possible, deployed with the help of financial tools.

Two more fun activities to go! We're gradually edging toward the end. Test your limits with a quick attempt at this one.

Fun Activity

Using hypothetical figures of $24,000 purchase price, $8,000 salvage value, and six-year useful life for your small business pickup truck, calculate the straight-line and double-declining balance depreciation for the asset. Remember that we have already used this example to demonstrate the sum-of-the-year's-digits method. Compare the depreciation outcomes of the three methods and give your verdict as to the factors that would influence your preference for any of the three methods.

Chapter Summary

- You are required to use recommended formulas to calculate depreciation and post the loss of value in the income statement and the balance sheet.
- The straight-line method is a simple approach to depreciation that involves apportioning an asset's loss of value to equal installments spread throughout its useful life.
- It is prudent to explore all depreciation methods and weigh each one of them against the particular asset you need to depreciate before selecting your preferred method.

In the next chapter you will learn the different methods for calculating amortization when performing the valuation of your intangible assets.

Chapter Eight:
Amortization

Chances are that you may have been involved in business acquisition negotiations. It could be that you were buying a business from another person, or selling yours to another person. Have you ever realized that goodwill valuation has always been contentious in such negotiations? From my own experience, people sometimes tend to exaggerate the valuation of their goodwill, licenses or any other intangible assets. This is simply because some people don't realize that these assets do lose value over time.

Amortization is similar to depreciation, the main difference here being that the former focuses on intangible assets. You are required to account for the annual dip in the valuation of all your intangible assets including trademarks, goodwill, patents, licenses, franchises, and copyrights.

The GAAP guidelines for amortization provide the simplest classification of intangible assets with reference to either their origins or duration of useful life. This means that your intangible asset could be classified in the purchased, internal creations, predictable life span, or indefinite lifespan categories. These categorizations are important in determining the assets that should be amortized or impaired.

When it comes to accounting for intangible assets, you are required to recognize only the initial cost of purchasing the asset. You cannot capitalize any other costs that you may incur internally in the development or upgrade of an intangible asset. And this is where the issue of internal creations comes to mind. Consideration of costs related to internal creations is permitted only in circumstances where they are IRS-issued exemptions. The aspect of the IRS exemptions for internal creations is discussed in greater detail later on in the chapter.

Be careful to not overlook the recommended thresholds when determining the historical cost and economic life of intangible assets. For example, there are times when you will be not using the useful life span parameter in your calculations when dealing with intangible assets that can be used for indefinite durations. In other words, you do not have to use a given parameter when it is difficult to derive an accurate estimation for that particular parameter.

You will find it easier to amortize an intangible asset that you have purchased or acquired because it has got a historical cost. Similarly, the availability of the useful life duration of an asset makes it easier for you to use the straight-line method. But it is not possible to use the straight-line method to amortize an intangible asset that does not have a definite economic life. As a general rule of the thumb, you will amortize intangible assets with predictable useful life spans and impair the ones with indefinite useful life spans. Unlike amortization, which focuses on historical cost and useful life, impairment focuses on the comparison between the fair value and the book value of the intangible asset in question.

How to Post Amortization Expense

Use the same procedure you applied in depreciation to account for amortization. The only difference will be the destination accounts.

Account	Debit	Credit
Amortization expense	$475.36	
Accumulated amortization		$475.36

Understanding the Different Types of Amortization

By now, it is pretty clear why the straight-line method (as discussed in the previous topic) would be the first choice for anyone seeking a simple approach to calculating amortization. Nonetheless, save for circumstances where the IRS requirements tie you to the straight-line method, be flexible to alternatives.

Straight-Line Amortization

The straight-line method of amortization is similar to the straight-line depreciation method, with the major difference being the nature of the assets in question. Intangible assets also tend to have longer useful life spans compared to tangible fixed assets. Residual value is not an important factor here because the straight-line method allocates the amortization cost until the value of the asset reduces to zero. Its formula simply involves dividing the historical cost by the asset's duration of useful life.

For example, assuming that you purchased a copyright that has a 15-year useful life at a cost of $2,700, the straight-line amortization for the asset will be $2,700/15 = $180. This calculation simply means you will be allocating $180 every year for 15 years as the amortization expense of the copyright. The value of the copyright will reduce to zero when you allocate the final $180 in the final year.

Therefore, you cannot use the straight-line method if you are not able to estimate the economic life of an intangible asset. However, there are exceptions where you can use the IRS-recommended useful life. The IRS (2020) recommends that you deploy the straight-line method, a useful life of 15 years, and zero residual value for select intangible items that have been in existence since January 1, 2004, and onwards.

It is common for the IRS to recommend the use of the straight-line method in certain circumstances when amortizing your intangibles. That is because the IRS wants to simplify the filing of your returns and this particular method is known to provide such convenience. It is also likely that such recommendations could be attached to certain compulsory tax filing requirements. Therefore, whenever you come across an IRS recommendation that you deploy the straight-line method, make sure you do it.

Income Forecast Amortization

Income forecast is an alternative method that you can use instead of the straight-line method to determine the amortization of your intangible assets. Multiply the historical cost of the asset by a fraction representing the net income that the asset has generated in the current accounting period and the overall projected income during its useful life. This means you have to estimate the total income that the asset will generate, usually over a period stretching a maximum of 10 taxable years, according to the IRS (2020).

For example, let's assume that a license you acquire for $1,000 a year ago has generated $200 in the first year and you are projecting that it will generate $200 per year for the remaining 9 taxable years. Your calculation for the income forecast amortization will be as follows.

$1,000 x $200 / [$200 + ($200 x 9)]

= $1,000 x 1/10

= $1,000 x 0.1

= $100

Therefore, the amortization for your license using the income forecast method will be $100. Interestingly, this is the same amortization cost you will incur if you were to use the straight line method—that is $1,000 / 10 months. The IRS (2020) actually recommends the use of this particular method as an alternative to the straight-line method when amortizing copyrights, patents, and books, as well as artistic works such as movies and music.

Quiz: Which of the following methods is applicable to both amortization and depreciation of assets?

a) Double-declining balance
b) Straight-line method
c) Units of production

How To Amortize Different Intangible Assets

To guide you through the process, I have discussed some of the common intangible assets and how they are affected by amortization.

Trademark

The trademark grants your business the exclusive rights to a name, brand, or logo. It is always important to use a trademark to protect your unique business identification parameters from being exploited by other businesses. The value of a trademark is based on the cost of its acquisition. This value is mostly generated by mergers and purchases of other businesses or brands. Absence of such growth dynamics results in a low trademark valuation. That is because any investments that you make internally, with respect to costs incurred to create or market a logo or brand name, do not count toward a trademark valuation. The trademark is impaired rather than amortized using the straight-line method because it belongs to the category of intangible assets that have indefinite useful life.

To account for the impairment cost of the trademark, post a journal entry debiting the amortization expense account and crediting the accumulated depreciation account. Also post a contra entry debiting the amount in the accumulated depreciation account and crediting the respective trademark account.

Copyright

A copyright provides you the legal backing for protecting your creative work from reproduction by other people without permission. This includes works of literature, software programs or any other work that you have authored. According to the IRS (2020), software tools that you have developed specifically for use in internal operations qualify for consideration as an amortizable intangible asset. You are allowed to account for the cost associated with the depletion of the value of such internally developed software over its useful life.

Although you are not supposed to capitalize internal creations, there are IRS exceptions that relate to copyrights. Indeed, the investment you committed towards creating a copyright counts towards its valuation. And if you acquired the copyright, you will value it on the basis of the purchase price. A copyright is amortized because it is possible to estimate its useful life.

To account for the amortization cost of the copyright, post a journal entry debiting the amortization expense account and crediting the accumulated depreciation account. Also post a contra entry debiting the amount in the accumulated depreciation account and crediting the respective copyright account.

Patent

Patenting is a legal measure that attributes the utilization or commercial rights of a particular invention to the inventor. You could be eligible for a utility, design, or plant patent depending on the nature of your invention. A patent has a lifespan of 20 years in the United States. This means that you will amortize your patent at the end of each accounting period until you exhaust its useful life.

To account for the amortization cost of the patent, post a journal entry debiting the amortization expense account and crediting the accumulated depreciation account. Also post a contra entry debiting the amount in the accumulated depreciation account and crediting the respective patent account.

Goodwill

Goodwill is the difference between the net value of assets, as reflected in the balance sheet, and the acquisition price tag of a business. Such goodwill usually arises when you acquire a business as a going concern on the basis of its market valuation. For example, Jane has a soft drinks distribution with $50,000 worth of stock, a pickup truck worth $15,000, refrigeration equipment worth $4,000, and a $14,200 outstanding business loan. Jane insists on selling you the business for $70,000 by virtue of its extensive distribution network. In this case, the net value of Jane's business will be $50,000 + $15,000 + $4,000 - $14,200 = $54,800. As such, the business will have a goodwill valuation of $70,000 - $54,800 = $15,200.

The excess value above the net value of assets is attributable to the track record relating to factors such as customer loyalty and brand recognition. You are required to review your goodwill valuation every fiscal year to test for impairment and account for any changes in its valuation. For goodwill to be positive, the fair value (or market value) attributable to the units in question must exceed their book value. Impairment occurs the moment the fair value dips below the book value. It is this loss of value that you will be accounting for in your accounting entries. The impairment cost is recognized as a loss in the income statement.

To account for the impairment of the goodwill, post a journal entry debiting the amortization expense account and crediting the accumulated depreciation account. Also post a contra entry debiting the amount in the accumulated depreciation account and crediting the respective goodwill account.

Licenses and Franchises

Franchising and licensing allows you to sell or distribute products on behalf of another business and vice versa. A large business that boasts an established brand name already may adopt an expansion strategy that involves franchising or licensing agreements with smaller businesses. If you enter such agreements, you will be free to use the branding and other protected marketing infrastructure of the franchisor or licensor. You have to amortize your franchise or license because it is possible to estimate its useful life.

To account for the amortization cost of franchising or licensing, post a journal entry debiting the amortization expense account and crediting the accumulated depreciation account. Also post a contra entry debiting the amount in the accumulated depreciation account and crediting the respective franchise or license account.

Legalities and Determinations

Legalities are the considerations that you should keep in mind when amortizing your intangibles. They largely dwell on the IRS guidelines and other government laws that you must comply with when interacting with the different parameters of amortization. The issue of determining the useful life of an intangible asset is particularly important, considering that some of these assets have indefinite life spans. This is where you will find the IRS provisions helpful in guiding you on how to determine the amortization procedures for different intangible assets.

As we have seen earlier in this chapter, there is an IRS (2020) recommendation that you deploy a useful life of 15 years and select intangible items whose useful life you cannot estimate. For example, how would you estimate the useful life of your membership to an organization such as a trade association? Well, it is almost impossible to make such estimations with certainty despite the fact that there are economic benefits associated with your membership to the association. That is the reason why the IRS has made this particular recommendation to take care of such situations. The recommendation actually affords you the flexibility to amortize assets in situations where alternative approaches such as impairment would not suffice.

However, there are certain exceptions to this rule. An intangible asset that was sold to you by another person will be not eligible for consideration. This also includes intangible assets whose useful life you can estimate with considerable accuracy. Intangible assets that have useful life spans that are insufficient to be considered for amortization as per the IRS guidelines are ineligible as well.

There are certain methods that you cannot apply in your calculations of amortization of certain intangibles. For example, the IRS (2020) bars you from deploying the MACRS method in the amortization of assets of artistic nature including movies, music and other recordings of audio and video content. The IRS recommends that you restrict your choice of an amortization method to either the straight-line or income forecast.

Patents and Copyrights

The IRS recommends the use of straight-line method to account for the amortization of intangible assets such as patents and copyrights. These recommendations focus mainly on the cost and useful life parameters of the assets. You will find the IRS guidelines useful if you find yourself stranded or confused about how to handle certain situations.

There are occasions when you will find yourself entangled in a dilemma about overlapping scenarios for determining the amortization of a patent or a copyright. For example, what happens when faced with a choice between the IRS-recommended useful life for a patent or a copyright and the remainder of the asset's useful life from the time of acquisition? Such is the dilemma that you would experience when you acquire an intangible asset that has exhausted a portion of its useful life.

The IRS sets the record straight about such scenarios. For example, you are allowed to select the lesser of the two when faced with a choice between the IRS-granted duration of useful life and the remainder of the useful life of the asset. The other important clarification concerning the IRS provisions is that you are at liberty to deduct the remainder of an intangible asset's cost in the event that it completely loses its value prior to the exhaustion of its useful life.

Computer Software

The IRS (2020) recommends that you use a straight-line method and a useful life of 36 months to amortize your computer software. However, amortization of computer software depends on whether or not it falls under section 197 of the IRS Code. If your computer software description falls under section 197, requirements for intangible assets, then it does not qualify for depreciation, according to the IRS (2020). Such a situation prevails if the computer software is a primary business or forms part of a business that you acquired.

Therefore there are no guarantees that you will always be able to amortize your computer software. The software must not be part of section 197 of the IRS Code. In addition, the software should be designated as an asset for sale to the general public, be void of licensing restrictions, and not subjected to significant modifications, according to the IRS (2020).

Purpose and Application to Tax Reporting

Amortization is meant to help you maintain the right valuation of your intangible assets. Failure to recognize the amortization expense will leave you with overstated and understated accounts. Your financial statements would simply be erroneous because your intangible assets will be overstated in the balance sheet, while your operations expenses will be understated in the income statement. For example, a patent that you have not subjected to amortization will inadvertently increase your income because you will not have made the appropriate expense entry for that particular item. This exposes you to higher taxes because you will not be able to access certain amortization allowances and deduction.

Your accounting entries for amortization have an impact on your tax reporting. You will report a lower tax if you incur a high amortization expense, and vice versa. That is because higher amortization expense would decrease both your income and tax liability, while lower amortization expense has the opposite impact. Scrutiny of your tax reporting procedures is important because there are certain IRS guidelines that you must observe to be able to file accurate tax returns for your business. There are occasions when the IRS could offer you benefits such as depreciation allowance, exemptions, and deductions for certain classes of amortizable intangible assets. It is worth exploring these benefits to cushion your business from high tax liabilities.

One more fun activity to go! As I did throughout this book, I want to be sure that you understood all the stuff I discussed in this chapter.

Fun Activity

Use the straight-line method to calculate the amortization of a $2,250 worth patent that Derrick purchased in March for his laboratory services business. The patent has a useful life of 15 years and does not have a residual value. Derrick's financial year ends on October 31.

Chapter Summary

- Amortization is the process of accounting for the diminishing value of your intangible assets, such as licenses, patents, goodwill, trademarks, and copyrights, over time.

- The IRS recommends the use of straight-line method to account for the amortization of intangible assets such as patents and copyrights.
- Your accounting entries for amortization have an impact on your tax reporting with respect to deductions and allowances.

In the next chapter you will learn about the importance of auditing your financial reports.

Chapter Nine:
Auditing

Auditing is designed to help you, or any other interested party, ascertain the true position of your business operations and strategy. The auditing process probes the accuracy of your financial information in addition to checking the authenticity of the procedures used to gather, process, and interpret your financial data. Issues of compliance with regulatory requirements are also paramount in the auditing process.

However, I've never understood why audits cause panic in businesses and other organizations. I too was a culprit during my days as a junior accountant. The arrival of external auditors was never good news; there was always tension and anxiety throughout the process. Anyway, let's discuss auditing in greater detail and understand why it's important.

Fundamentals of Small Business Auditing

Publicly listed companies are required by law to have their accounts audited annually by an external party or entity. As for small businesses, auditing is more or less a voluntary exercise unless it is sanctioned by the IRS. Having auditing knowledge is important because you could choose to conduct the exercise by yourself or be in a better position to track the entire procedure if it is done by someone else.

Auditing is not as complex as it may sound, but it could become difficult if some of your accounting records are missing or manipulated. Much of the auditing process actually focuses on your physical and/or electronic records. Therefore, the auditor would be looking at the cash receipts, accounts receivables invoices and aging debtors listing, accounts payable invoices and aging creditors listing, credit notes, debit notes, inventory, and schedule of fixed assets and long-term liabilities, among other financial records. The auditor must have unfettered access to both the electronic and physical records. This means providing the auditor login access to your accounting system and providing the support required to access crucial documents.

The auditor's verdict is contained in the audit report. The auditor will give your small business either a clean bill of health or issue a negative opinion depending on the findings of the auditing process. You will definitely attract the auditor's wrath if there are glaring inconsistencies and inaccurate entries in your financial records. The auditing report also summarizes the auditor's perspectives about the scope and objectives of the entire auditing process.

Contrary to commonly held perceptions, auditing is actually beneficial to your small business in many ways. Specifically, it has the potential of detecting weaknesses and threats that derail growth. As much as you may have a hint about pilferage or fraud affecting your small business, you may never understand their full impact until you carry out a substantive evaluation. This way, you can seal loopholes to enhance efficiency and increase productivity.

The practice of auditing your business accounts every year also creates confidence among your investors, lenders, and suppliers. Having audited accounts for your small business also makes it convenient for you to pursue and acquire certain certifications like the ISO. It will also be easier for you to file your tax returns and spare yourself the worries of attracting the dreaded IRS audit when you have certified audited accounts in place. Your audited accounts are also important points of reference for your insurance service providers. The information in the audited accounts helps insurers determine the accurate valuation of your small business and calculate your premiums.

Internal Audit
Internal or self audit is essentially an in-house mechanism for examining your accounting activities. Although internally audited accounts are primarily for

use in your own decision-making processes, they help raise your business profile to your stakeholders. Whereas it is the norm for large businesses to have well-staffed internal auditing departments, a small business would be capable of employing one or two individuals to perform the auditing function. An internal auditor should be able to produce periodic reports on short notice because theirs is more or less a full time job.

Having auditing staff transforms internal auditing into a continuous process that allows you to identify operational or strategic gaps in advance. For example, an internal audit could help you unravel the mystery behind a sudden dip or stagnation of your monthly collections. When it comes to strategic investments, such as newly installed payroll accounting systems, an internal audit will reveal the causes of any implementation challenges that you might experience. In addition to tracking all the financial aspects of your business, the internal auditing also examines other factors in the business environment that must be observed to achieve stable growth. Issues of regulation, such as compliance to federal rules and state bylaws, must rank high in an internal auditor's list of priorities.

External Audit

External auditing is not a prerogative of large firms. There are many occasions where you may be required to present independently audited accounts of your small business. For example, certain lenders will specifically request for your externally audited accounts for you to be able to conduct any business with them. As discussed earlier in this chapter, audited accounts are crucial for acquiring certifications. For your information, the issuance of these certifications prioritizes externally audited accounts over internally audited accounts.

Deloitte & Touche, Ernst & Young (EY), KPMG, and PricewaterhouseCoopers (PwC) are the best known auditing firms, thanks to their many years of existence and global operations networks. Contracting such renowned brands lends greater credibility to your audited financial reports. However, services associated with these big four audit firms come at a cost because of higher fees for their services. Your audited financial reports will always pass the credibility test, as long as it is duly performed by an accredited or certified audit firm. The best approach is to contract an auditing firm that is within range of your budget estimation for audit services.

External auditing is considered to be more objective compared to internal auditing, which can be biased and prone to interference. Being an outsider, it is unlikely that an independent auditor will have a conflict of interest when performing duties. This is unlike an internal auditor, whose loyalty lies with the business that they are responsible for examining. Independent auditing reinforces the requirement to perform an impartial review of your financial information and disclose all the material facts about the business.

However, the independence of an external auditor is not always guaranteed. The enactment of the Sarbanes-Oxley Act 2002 was specifically caused by blatant financial manipulations that characterized the collapse of the Enron Corporation. The Act was enacted to curb, among other problems, the collusion between external auditors and their clients, as was witnessed in Enron's unceremonious collapse in 2001. For example, Enron used unorthodox accounting methods for many years to hide ballooning debts and toxic investments from unsuspecting investors.

Enron's external auditor, Arthur Andersen LLP, always gave the company's financial accounts a clean bill of health despite the glaring accounting anomalies. It later emerged that Arthur Andersen's partner responsible for auditing Enron accounts, David B. Duncan, was an accomplice to the fraud. In fact, upon learning the news that Enron was under the radar of the SEC, Duncan attempted to destroy the paper trail by shredding tons of documents associated with Enron's accounts (Oppel Jr. & Eichenwald, 2002). This revelation got Duncan fired by Arthur Andersen. But Arthur Andersen did not survive this scandal either and it collapsed soon after Enron's demise.

The Enron experience just shows how delicate and ugly external auditing can get. Although this scandal occurred in a stock exchange listed company, you cannot rule out the possibility of such fraud rocking your small business. Such collusion incidences between staff and auditors are common even in small business organizations. This calls for caution on your part when selecting and working with independent auditors.

Types of External Auditing Verdicts

The production of a report is the final responsibility of the external auditor. This report is usually modeled on the provisions of the GAAP. The auditor's opinion is one of the key items of the audit report. In fact, the opinion is considered to be the most important outcome of the audit report because it is the final verdict about the auditor's findings. An audit opinion may be unqualified, qualified, or adverse (Grigg, 2020).

Unqualified opinion is a stamp of approval of the accuracy of the financial information of your business. An auditor issues unqualified opinions upon satisfaction that all the material facts are representative of the true position of the business. Qualified opinion, on the other hand, is an auditor's way to show that they were dissatisfied with the manner the audit was conducted. In other words, a qualified opinion simply means that the audit, although complete, did not meet the recommended thresholds. Qualified opinion can be occasioned by incidents such as insufficient documentation or limited access to information for the auditor to be able to pass a conclusive verdict.

Adverse opinion arises when the auditor is convinced beyond doubt that the material facts presented in the financial reports are misleading and unrepresentative of the true position of the business. Such an opinion means your business has completely failed the audit.

Quiz: What type of opinion will an external auditor issue if your financial statements are found to be accurate and reflecting the true position of your small business?

a) Adverse opinion
b) Unqualified opinion
c) Qualified opinion

The IRS Audit

The IRS audit primarily seeks to address discrepancies between your tax filing and financial records. Once your business gets on the IRS' radar, there is no escape. This happens when the IRS detects errors in your tax filing. The IRS will want to look into your current tax returns and compare them with your returns for the past three years to establish the trends and accuracy of your filings.

If you are lucky, the IRS will seek to sort out your tax issue through correspondence. Once you receive the IRS letter with audit queries, you simply respond to the queries and mail the letter and copies of relevant supporting documents back to the IRS. The process will end at this point if the IRS is satisfied with your responses. However, the IRS will launch a field audit if it finds the need to probe your business further. This could take place at your business premises or any other appropriate location identified by the IRS.

Tips for Avoiding IRS Scrutiny

The IRS audit is one of the processes that you should dread as a small business owner, and there are good reasons behind that warning. Given that your business is small, it takes something extraordinary for the IRS to detect fault in your financial reports. Therefore, the IRS will simply be implying that there is something wrong with your financial reporting the moment it sanctions an audit of your small business. The onus will be on you to prove that you did nothing wrong during the audit. There is a heavy price to pay if the audit proves that the concerns of the IRS are right. The slightest sign of suspicion will prompt the IRS to swing into action and launch an audit to evaluate every single aspect of your small business strategy and operations.

There are numerous reasons that may prompt the IRS to launch audits of small businesses. For example, filing losses every year can raise an alarm. Reporting losses in consecutive years is bound to attract the attention of the IRS. Frequent losses will still bring your business into sharp focus even if your reported losses do not occur in consecutive years. Reporting losses in three out of five years will definitely raise eyebrows and increase the chances of your small business being subjected to an IRS audit. Make sure that your financial report reflects the true position of your small business to avoid such an eventuality.

The desire to lower your tax liability could tempt you to file excessive claims for deductions. It is common for small business owners to find the slightest excuse to list a business expense as a deduction claim. This is one mistake that you should avoid at all costs because that amounts to issuing an open invite to the IRS. Restrict your deduction claims to qualifying expenses for which you have documentary evidence. Changes to your deduction claims should be gradual and consistent. A sharp rise in the amount of your deduction claims is one of the signals of tax fraud that the IRS will look out for when analyzing your tax filings.

Cash remains the most favored form of transactions, especially among small businesses. Cash receipts and cash payments are routine modes of conducting business and you would ordinarily not expect to attract anyone's attention over such aspects of your business operations. However, a transaction could land you in trouble with the IRS if you cannot verify the sources of the cash. That's why it is always important to capture your cash sales records in your cash sale receipts book or point of sale system. Large cash transactions for payments and purchases would also spell doom for your small business. Use a combination of payments systems, such as credit/debit cards, electronic payments, and online payments to be on the safe side. Also avoid selling or purchasing fixed assets with cash.

In the world of accounting, rounded numbers are usually the easiest to detect when analyzing the financial reports of a small business. Such numbers act as leads for detecting fraud in financial reports. For example, too many rounded figures such as $1,200,

$3,400, $10,000, or 15,500 will always look suspect in your financial reports. Therefore, it will not require an effort for the IRS to detect such suspect figures and place your business on the radar. Do not round off decimal points to whole numbers. Always retain the decimal points the way they appear in your calculations.

The timing of your tax filings is very important if you want to remain in the IRS' good books. You must file your tax returns on time every year. It is understandable that there could be one or two occasions when you could fail to meet the deadline for filing returns due to circumstances beyond your control. But that should never be the mode of operation in your business. Late filing of returns will prompt the IRS to subject your business to an audit to probe your operations.

Inaccurate reporting of your taxable income would be a recipe to disaster when it comes to all matters IRS. You must report all the taxable income that you earned within the U.S. and its territories during the accounting period. It doesn't matter whether or not your accounts are held within the country. All your taxable income must be reflected in your filing of tax returns regardless of the location of your bank account. The rule of the thumb when preparing your taxable income summaries is to avoid understating the money you earned from your business activities during the reporting period.

The IRS will also want to audit your accounts if it detects suspicious deductibles that point to misuse of certain fixed assets, such as automobiles. For example, chances are high that the IRS will want to scrutinize your accounts if your deduction claims include the use of your vehicle to carry out activities that are not related to your business operations. For example, you would be inviting trouble if you file a deduction claim for use of your vehicle to take friends to a party. Restrict your deduction claims to business-related activities in your tax returns to be on the safe side.

Tips for Embracing an IRS Audit

Although it is advisable to avoid it if you can by filing accurate returns, you may find yourself on the IRS' radar one way or another. An IRS audit does not mean that you have necessarily committed fraud. It is normal to commit errors of omission or commission unknowingly; such errors can always be explained. The IRS will just want you to set the record straight about certain erroneous entries.

You have nothing to worry about an IRS audit as long as the errors that triggered it were not intentional. Therefore, an IRS audit is not necessarily a bad thing. You should embrace it if it comes your way by providing all the necessary information that an IRS auditor or agent will request. Make sure that you grant the auditor unfettered access to your financial records and accounting systems. Learn to be calm throughout the process and don't fear to ask the auditor questions or seek clarifications about aspects of the process.

Audit Planning

There are universal procedures that a professional auditor will follow throughout the process. Sending notifications to the relevant stakeholders, developing schedule, planning, and reporting the audit are extremely important for both internal and external audits. In an external audit, the independent auditing party is expected to follow proper planning guidelines that will facilitate efficiency, thoroughness, and impartiality.

The audit plan describes the tasks that the auditor will perform from the beginning to the end with the objective of delivering a binding verdict. It highlights the underlying motivations and establishes the scope of the audit. There are recommended procedures for planning an internal audit. The Institute of Internal Auditors actually serves as a reference point for developing an effective audit plan.

How to Conduct Internal Audit

Has the idea of conducting an internal audit for your small business by yourself ever crossed your mind? Maybe this is one of the areas that you may prefer to leave to your internal auditor or another accounting professional. Given the many responsibilities that you shoulder in managing your business operations and strategy, it is unlikely that you will find the time to conduct a professional-level audit by yourself. However, it is possible to conduct a basic audit that will help you gauge the state of your business operations. The key steps that you will follow in your audit will revolve around the issues of system compliance, effectiveness, efficiency, and transformation.

- Step One: Evaluate your system to find out if it is in sync with the laid down procedures and overall profile of the business. You will be comparing the procedures that the system prescribes against the routine activities in your business to find out if there are any discrepancies. There should be compliance between what the system says and actual operations. For example, if the system specifies that workdays should begin at 9 a.m. and end at 4 p.m., that is what should be happening. If the internal audit proves otherwise, it will be a signal that your system is not compliant and urgent measures are needed to fix the anomaly.

- Step Two: Examine the effectiveness of your system and its capacity to deliver on your target operations and strategic objectives. There are various broad areas that you will be examining including inventory management, IT equipment and tools, workplace safety, customer care, payroll system, and employee training, among others. Prevalence of loopholes in any of the functional areas of your system will suggest the need for a review to address existing problems.

- Step Three: Review the efficiency of your system with respect to its output relative to the resources that you put into the system. It is actually an analysis of whether the output of your system is worth the investment that you have made. An efficient system is one that delivers fast and satisfactory results at minimum costs. As such, you will be looking at different operational parameters to determine if they are facilitative or detrimental to your efficiency objectives. For example, there could be numerous complaints from customers about the time it takes customer support to respond to their queries. In this case, you will want to find out whether the problem lies with your team or your customer support management tools. Your internal audit should reveal the exact problem.

- Step Four: Prepare a report of your findings. The report should identify all the incompliant, ineffective, and inefficient areas. Prescribe remedial measures for each of the problems as identified in the first three steps of the audit process.

Hurray! We're finally there. My final chapter exercise for you. Give it a try!

Fun Activity

The so-called Big Four auditors, comprising Deloitte, EY, KPMG, and PwC are highly respected in auditing circles and are well known for their delivery of quality services. Why would you prioritize any of these audit firms over smaller firms in your search for an external auditor?

Chapter Summary

- It is important to audit your accounts to be able to gauge the progress of your business operations and the impact of your growth strategy.
- Internal auditing is an in-house mechanism for examining your accounting and financial reporting activities.
- Externally audited accounts carry more weight compared to internally audited accounts when dealing with lenders, investors, government agencies, and other stakeholders.

Answers to Fun Activities

Here are the answers to the questions that I posed to you at the end of each chapter. I hope you enjoyed every bit of these exercises. They were definitely fun for me to write!

Chapter One Fun Activity

I guess this one was quite simple, wasn't it?

Inventory purchase on credit:

Debit	$1,640 to inventory	Asset increase
Credit	$1,640 to creditors	Liability increase

Cash sale of industrial detergents:

Debit	$745 to cash	Asset increase
Credit	$745 to inventory	Asset decrease

Chapter Two Fun Activity

How did you find this one? I hope you enjoyed every bit of it. Anyway, the matching principle concerns the ability to match the projected income against the projected expenses in a particular accounting period. That's because accrual basis accounting allows you to recognize revenue upon the issuance of a sales invoice and expenses upon receipt of a purchase invoice. Therefore, the matching principle helps you predict the income that you will earn in a particular period by determining the difference between the projected revenue and expenses.

Chapter Three Fun Activity

I know this one may have left you sweating. It's not that difficult anyway, especially if you followed the budgeting steps I shared with you in the chapter. Take a look at the answer, and I am sure you will agree!

Arcwvl Agencies
Cash Budget
For the Period Ending December 31, 2020
January 1, 2020

	Quarter One	Quarter Two	Quarter Three	Quarter Four	Annual
Opening cash balance (Bal b/f)	2,500.00	2,900.00	2,068.00	10,478.00	2,500.00
Add receipts from cash sale	17,800.00	31,250.00	29,320.00	38,420.00	119,790.00
Period's total cash	**20,300.00**	**34,150.00**	**31,388.00**	**48,898.00**	**122,290.00**
Less cash expenses					
Raw materials	-9,800.00	-12,430.00	-11,940.00	-14,785.00	-48,955.00
Labor	-4,500.00	-6,100.00	-5,820.00	-7,200.00	-23,620.00
Distribution expenses	-2,800.00	-5,820.00	-3,450.00	-4,700.00	-16,770.00
Equipment lease	-4,800.00	-6,500.00	-6,200.00	-4,000.00	-21,500.00
Total cash expenses	-21,900.00	-30,850.00	-27,410.00	-30,685.00	-110,845.00
Budget surplus/deficit	**1,600.00**	**3,300.00**	**3,978.00**	**18,213.00**	**11,445.00**
Financing activities					
loans	4,500.00		6,500.00		11,000.00
loan repayment		-1,100.00		-1,800.00	-2,900.00
Interest on loans		-132.00		-216.00	-348.00
Net financing activities	4,500.00	-1,232.00	6,500.00	-2,016.00	7,752.00
Closing cash balance (Bal c/f)	2,900.00	2,068.00	10,478.00	16,197.00	3,693.00

The opening balance is the balance carried over from the previous period, while closing balance is the remainder of your cash that you carry over to the next period. The opening balance for the year (annual) is similar to the opening balance of the first quarter because they both represent the beginning of the budget period. In this particular example, we have a budget deficit in the first quarter and budget surpluses in the other three quarters. Arcwyl Agencies borrowed $4,500 to cover the deficit.

Chapter Four Fun Activity

I have no doubt that this one must have been an easy one to solve! All the same, the statement of cash flows has three segments that include cash flows from operating activities, cash flows from financing activities, and cash flows from investing activities. The segmentation helps pool cash inflows and outflows according to their sources and purpose. This makes it easier for you to recognize income from different sources and to take a balanced approach in the allocation of your spending to different activities in your business. It is also important to match cash inflows and outflows accordingly to avoid setbacks in your operations and planning. For example, spending cash meant for operations on investments will cripple your operations due to deficits of cash inflows because investments are not meant to generate income over the short term.

Chapter Five Fun Activity

For those of us that love accounting calculations, this must have been so easy. If you take a look at the sample balance sheet in Chapter Four, it has the following details:

Total current assets = $61,590.00
Total current liabilities = $58,094.00
Working capital = current assets/current liabilities
= $61590.00 / $58094.00 = 1.06

This is a positive working capital that signals favorable tidings for this particular business because a current ratio of 1.06 means the current assets are worth more than the liabilities. The situation would be opposite if the ratio was below 1. However, more needs to be done in terms of expanding the working capital by increasing output and minimizing costs of the short-term activities. This is achievable through initiatives such as increased marketing and operations efficiencies.

Chapter Six Fun Activity

I loved this one! Cost saving is the obvious reason that will sway you to choose free accounting software over paid software. It could be that your business is a startup and cannot afford a paid software tool at the moment. For an established small business that has been around for a while, other pressing priorities could prompt you to go for the free software tools. There is nothing wrong using free software as long as it serves the intended purpose. Tools such as Wave and Zipbooks have been around as free platforms for a while and they are widely used by small businesses. However, you should be prepared to miss out on certain advanced features and capabilities that come with paid tools. It is also important to examine the security credentials of your chosen free tools. It is common to come across software tools that do not provide sufficient protection to your business data.

Chapter Seven Fun Activity

So many numbers involved here, I know. But that's what accounting is all about! You will always enjoy it as you gradually get used to it. Anyway, let's crunch the numbers.

Calculation of the solution using the straight-line depreciation method is as follows:

Historical cost − salvage value ÷ useful life
= ($24,000 - $8,000) ÷ 6
= $2,666.67

Therefore, the pickup truck will be subjected to a depreciation charge of $2,666.67 equal installments for six years.

Calculation of the solution using the double-declining balance method is as follows:

Depreciation rate of the straight-line method: 100% ÷ 6 = 16.7%
Depreciation in year one: (16.7% x 2) x $24,000 = 33.4 ÷ 100 x $24,000 = $8,016

Book value in year two: $24,000 - $8,016 = $15,984
Depreciation in year two: (16.7% x 2) x $15,984 = 33.4 ÷ 100 x $15,984 = $5,338.66

Book value in year three: $15,984 - $5,338.66 = $10,645.34
Depreciation in year three: (16.7% x 2) x $10,645.34 = 33.4 ÷ 100 x $10,645.34 = $3,555.54

Book value in year four: $10,645.34 - $3,555.54 = 7,089.80
Depreciation in year four: (16.7% x 2) x $7,089.80 = 33.4 ÷ 100 x $7,089.80 = $2,367.99

Book value in year five: $7,089.80 - $2,367.99 = $4,721.81
Depreciation in year five: (16.7% x 2) x $4,721.81 = 33.4 ÷ 100 x $4,721.81 = $1,577.08

Book value in year six: $4,721.81 - $1,577.08 = $3,144.73
Depreciation in year six: (16.7% x 2) x $3,144.73 = 33.4 ÷ 100 x $3,144.73 = $1,050.34

The key point to remember here is that salvage value does not count toward the determination of depreciation when using the double-declining balance method. You will depreciate the entire historical value of the asset on some occasions and be left with some balance of the valuation on other occasions.

The factors that would influence your choice of any of any particular depreciation method revolve around the issue of simplicity, individual motivation, and IRS recommendations. For example, the straight-line method always stands out as a simple method that is convenient for use in small businesses. However, the double-declining balance method would be the obvious choice if you are fueled by the motivation to cut your tax liability by allocating higher depreciation rates to the initial years of an asset's acquisition. When the IRS specifies a method that you should use to depreciate a particular fixed asset, you will have no choice but to adhere to that requirement.

Chapter Eight Fun Activity

Another easy one right there! Since Derrick's patent does not have a residual value, amortization for the intangible asset under the straight-line method will be $2,250/15 = $150. However, since he purchased the patent four months into the financial year, the depreciation for the first year will be $150 x 8/12 = $100.

Chapter Nine Fun Activity

Hope this one didn't send you spinning! Credibility is one of the obvious motivations that would prompt you to choose a big four audit firm over smaller firms. It is easier for investors, creditors, customers, and government agencies to have confidence in audited financial statements that have been approved by an audit partner associated with any of the Big Four firms. Therefore the use of any of the Big Four will raise the overall profile of your small business because they are well known and have good reputations.

However, the use of a big name audit firm does not necessarily guarantee credibility in auditing. The Enron case, discussed in this chapter, is one of the best examples of susceptibility of auditors to collude with members of client organizations. Arthur Andersen LLP was a big time audit firm that was at its prime when the Enron scandal erupted. It is clear that the reputation of the firm did not stop its auditing partner from committing fraud. The long and short of it is that you should always follow the auditing process closely regardless of the size or reputation of the audit firm. It is possible for an auditor to collude with your employees to compromise the accuracy of your financial reports.

Final Words

I am glad that I have been able to guide you through the different phases of accounting. As I stated in the introduction, I wrote this book to address your specific needs as a small business owner. The book has taken you through that journey, beginning with the basics of accounting for small businesses. I did emphasize to you that bookkeeping and the recording of transaction entries is where the accounting process begins. We also looked at the GAAP and the scope of its relevance to small businesses.

Budgeting and finance is the other area that this book prioritized to help you understand the planning aspect of business management. This goes hand in hand with the financial statements and financial analysis discussions of Chapters Four and Five, respectively. Your interaction with these three chapters has exposed you to very important tips about financial management in small business organizations.

The discussion of accounting software assistance in Chapter Six was equally important in this digital era. It is good to keep pace with the technological transformations in the management of your small business. Chapters Seven and Eight provide deep insights into the processes involved in accounting for the loss of value of your fixed tangible assets and intangible assets. You should be able to now calculate both depreciation and amortization in addition to posting the relevant journal entries. The in-depth discussion of auditing in Chapter Nine has demonstrated its significance to small businesses like yours. You now understand the trouble that fraud and skewed financial reporting could bring.

Thank yourself for taking the initiative to read this book because it has helped you overcome challenges associated with accounting in small businesses. Past research has shown that accounting remains one of the major challenges that US small businesses experience year after year. Let's take some insights into some findings of the Wasp Barcode Technologies report (2015) to better understand the significance of accounting in your small business. The management of revenue, or collections, was the top ranking challenge in accounting with 51 percent prevalence among the respondents (Wasp Barcode Technologies, 2015). According to the report, other challenges were cash flow management (44 percent), paperwork processing (33 percent), periodical closing of books of accounts (28 percent), and payroll management (27 percent).

Revenue generation will always be a top ranking challenge if you have a startup business that is seeking traction for its products in the market. It is also a challenge if your business has been around for a while but cannot cope with market competition or debt collection. Your business will not be able to meet its financial obligations if the goods or services you have sold on credit are not paid for in good time. You can now see why the accounting knowledge you have acquired will be helpful when you need to fast track revenue collection.

Paperwork processing entails preparation, distribution, and storage of documentation relating to expenses and revenues. The fact that 33 percent of the pooled respondents identified document processing as one of their biggest challenges raises concerns. Poor management of document processing is a recipe for disaster because it exposes your business to operational inefficiencies.

Periodical closing of the books is an important procedure that you need to perform at the end of every accounting period. It ensures seamless transition to the next accounting period. You will ideally be removing any amounts from temporary accounts—that is, income and expense accounts, so as to begin the next accounting period with zero balances. The process involves making closing entries that move the end of period balances from the income statement to the balance sheet. This accounting process ensures that you will have only current entries in your income statement for the current period.

Payroll management was the other key area identified by polled respondents in the Wasp Barcode Technologies (2015) survey. I addressed the issue in great detail in the book and you now know how to go about it.

I thank you for the effort you have made to acquire accounting skills. I believe all the information and tips I shared with you were helpful. Let this book remain your companion. You can always keep referring back to the book whenever you need clarifications about certain issues.

A SPENDER'S
– GUIDE TO –
SAVING

At some point in their life, almost every adult has questioned where they will find a down payment for their house, or how they will finance their children's college tuition.

However, what's even more frightening are the situations that we cannot predict. If there is one thing that people have learned from the COVID-19 pandemic, it's that we can never fully predict what is going to happen. In December 2019, who would have predicted that only a few months later, millions of people across the world would lose their jobs? For that exact reason, having savings to catch you when you fall is absolutely essential.

The thought of reducing your spending to achieve a financial goal can be overwhelming. Therefore, A Spender's Guide to Saving will teach you the simple steps you need to know in order to put an end to the sleepless nights.

ISBN 9798656325929

90000

9 798656 325929

Leave a Review

As an independent author with a small marketing budget, reviews are my livelihood on this platform. If you enjoyed this book, I'd appreciate it if you could leave your honest feedback. You can do so by clicking the link below. I love hearing from my readers and I read every single review.

Link to review Page

References

Accounting.com. (n.d). What is GAAP? Retrieved March 24, 2020, from
https://www.accounting.com/resources/gaap/.

AICPA. (n.d). Financial Reporting Framework for SMEs. Retrieved March 24, 2020, from
https://www.aicpa.org/interestareas/frc/accountingfinancialreporting/pcfr.html.

Andriole, S. (2016, April 1). 10 Reasons Why Entrepreneurs Fail. *Forbes*.
https://www.forbes.com/sites/steveandriole/2016/04/01/10-reasons-why-entrepreneurs-fail/#537f6ca042d9.

Arline, K. (2017, June 13). GAAP: Standard & Rules for Accountants. *Business News Daily*.
Retrieved March 24, 2020, from
https://www.businessnewsdaily.com/5486-generally-accepted-accounting-principles-gaap.html.

Boyd, K, et. al. (n.d). Methods for Preparing Statements of the Cash Flows. *Dummies*. Retrieved
March 26, 2020, from
https://www.dummies.com/business/accounting/methods-for-preparing-the-statement-of-cash-flows/.

Carlson, R. (2020, February 25). The Difference Between Bookkeeping and Accounting in Small
Business. *The Balanced Small Business*. Retrieved March 24, 2020, from
https://www.thebalancesmb.com/bookkeeping-and-accounting-for-small-business-393002.

CFI Education Inc. (n.d). Working Capital Formula. Retrieved from March 26, 2020,
https://corporatefinanceinstitute.com/resources/knowledge/modeling/working-capital-for
mula/.

Flint, M. (2018, November, 8). Cash Flow: The Reason 82% of Small Businesses Fail. *Preferred
CFO*. Retrieved March 25, 2020, from
https://www.preferredcfo.com/cash-flow-reason-small-businesses-fail/.

Gigante, M. (2018, December 11). 30+ Important Accounting Statistics You Need to Know in
2019. *Learning Hub*. Retrieved, March 29, 2020, from
https://learn.g2.com/accounting-statistics.

Grigg, B.A. (2020, January 30). What is a Small Business Audit, and What Types of Audits
Should you be Ready For? *Fundera*. Retrieved March 24, 2020, from
https://www.fundera.com/blog/small-business-audit.

Hood, E. (2018, January 30). 13 Red Flags that Will Get Your Small Business Audited. Ignite

Spot. Retrieved March 29, 2020,from
http://blog.ignitespot.com/13-red-flags-that-will-get-your-small-businesses-audited.

IRS. (2020, March 24). Publication 946 (2019), How to Depreciate Property. Retrieved March
    29, 2020, from https://www.irs.gov/publications/p946.

Karpe, H. (2018, December 21). Personnel Costs – Formula, Procedure, and Method. *Business
    Guide Blog*. Retrieved April 2, 2020, from
    https://www.businessguideblog.com/calculate-personnel-costs/.

Lebaton, S. (2006, December 17). A Push to Fix the Fix on Wall Street. *The New York Times*.
    Retrieved April 2, 2020, from
    https://www.nytimes.com/2006/12/17/weekinreview/17labaton.html.

Loughran, M. (n.d). Depreciation Methods. *Dummies*. Retrieved April 5, 2020, from
    https://www.dummies.com/business/accounting/depreciation-methods/.

Lumen. (n.d). Introduction to Intangible Assets. Retrieved April 5, 2020, from
    https://courses.lumenlearning.com/boundless-accounting/chapter/introduction-to-intangible-assets/.

McIntyre, G. (2018, April 11). What Percent of Small Businesses Fail? And Other
> Need-to-Know Stats. *Fundera*. Retrieved on April 25, 2020, from
> https://www.fundera.com/blog/what-percentage-of-small-businesses-fail.

Naylor, T.J. (2014, April 3). How the Arthur Andersen and Enron Fraud Changed Accounting
> Forever. *Benzinga*. Retrieved March 29, 2020, from
> https://www.benzinga.com/general/education/14/04/4429482/how-the-arthur-anderson-and-e
> nron-fraud-changed-accounting-forever.

Oppel Jr., R.A. (2002, January 16). Enron's Collapse: The Overview; Arthur Andersen Fires an
> Executive for Enron Orders. *The New York Times*. Retrieved March 29, 2020, from
> https://www.nytimes.com/2002/01/16/business/enrons-collapse-overview-arthur-andersen-fi
> res-executive-for-enron-orders.html.

Pruitt, P. (2016, September 9). Reinventing Yourself: Life After a Business Failure.
> *Entrepreneur*. Retrieved on April 25, 2020, from
> https://www.entrepreneur.com/article/281251.

Sangster, A (2015). *Business Accounting* (13th Edition). London, United Kingdom: Pearson
> Education.

Yakal. K. (2020, January 12). The Best Small Business
Accounting Software for 2020. *PC*
    Magazine Digital Edition. Retrieved April 2, 2020,
from
    https://www.pcmag.com/picks/the-best-small-
business-accounting-software.

Waits, A. (n.d). Your Essential Guide to Effective
Inventory Management + 18 Techniques You
    Need to Know. *BigCommerce*. Retrieved March
26,2020, from
    https://www.bigcommerce.com/blog/inventory-
management/#common-inventory-managem
        ent-questions.

Wallace, D. (2013, March 25). Infographic: The Most
Tried and Failed Small Businesses. Small
    Biz Trends. Retrieved on April 25, 2020, from
    https://smallbiztrends.com/2013/03/infographic-failed-
small-businesses.html.

Warnes, B. (2020, March 4). What is Depreciation? And
How Do You Calculate It? *Bench*.
    Retrieved April 5, 2020, from
https://bench.co/blog/tax-tips/depreciation/.

Wasp Barcode Technologies. (2015). Small Business
Report – Accounting. Retrieved March 25,
    2020, from http://www.waspbarcode.com/small-
business-report-accounting.